Microsoft SharePoint 2013 Disaster Recovery Guide

Learn everything you need to know to design and implement a solid disaster recovery plan for SharePoint 2013

Peter Ward

Peter Abreu

Pavlo Andrushkiw

Pat Esposito

Jeff Gellman

Joel Plaut

[PACKT] enterprise

PUBLISHING   professional expertise distilled

BIRMINGHAM - MUMBAI

Microsoft SharePoint 2013 Disaster Recovery Guide

First published: September 2013

Production Reference: 1160913

Published by Packt Publishing Ltd.
Livery Place
35 Livery Street
Birmingham B3 2PB, UK.
ISBN 978-1-84968-510-8

www.packtpub.com

Cover Image by William Kewley (william.kewley@kbbs.ie)

Credits

Authors
Peter Ward
Peter Abreu
Pavlo Andrushkiw
Pat Esposito
Jeff Gellman
Joel Plaut

Reviewers
Stefan Goßner
Sothilingam Jeyashanker
Michael Nemtsev
Doug Ortiz
Richard Paterson
Daniele Proietti
Mikhail Pushin

Acquisition Editor
Kevin Colaco

Lead Technical Editor
Azharuddin Sheikh

Technical Editors
Shashank Desai
Sandeep Madnaik
Larissa Pinto
Aman Preet Singh

Project Coordinator
Anugya Khurana

Proofreader
Dirk Manuel

Indexer
Priya Subramani

Graphics
Valentina Dsilva
Ronak Dhruv
Disha Haria

Production Coordinator
Kyle Albuquerque

Cover Work
Kyle Albuquerque

Foreword

In my experience, the most significant challenge with enterprise implementations of SharePoint is that, while its usage and adoption is viral, it is often not given the same careful thought and planning as other enterprise technology investments.

When you implement technology within an enterprise that has significant up-front investment, such as an Enterprise Resource Planning (ERP) system, you do significant up-front planning. This up-front planning includes staffing appropriate teams and determining how to budget for the costs you know the technology investment will require for being successful. In other words, plan to ensure that IT can support and measure business utilization to meet the needs of the business over time. When you invest more than a million dollars in that same ERP technology, you can assume that careful thought has been given on how that ERP technology will remain up and running. This includes appropriate backups, fire drills, additional redundancy, and that it definitely includes technology configuration planning. SharePoint often sneaks in with a much smaller up-front investment—it's easy to see why it may not have the same diligence when it comes to availability and performance planning that the larger upfront technology investments (like ERPs) have.

Many SharePoint implementations start in a pilot, often driven by a few key passionate leaders—the eventual usage of the platform is varied in both its application and in its configuration as it grows and scales to meet increasing business needs. Eventually, you look back at the SharePoint investment and wonder how you got to the point you are at—where there are numerous dependencies and significant complexities. Then you are faced with that dreaded question (or worse, an actual disaster scenario) and someone asks—how do we get SharePoint back up and running?

The difference in why this is so challenging for SharePoint stems from the fact that what SharePoint does is as varied in organization usage as the numerous configurations of sites and settings you can implement. In one organization, they may be using SharePoint for basic team collaboration. In another, it may be used to surface complex dashboards or connect other systems. This variation makes planning for things such as availability, redundancy, and disaster recovery a significant challenge.

Nowhere is this more apparent than when you look at disaster recovery strategies for SharePoint, and find confusion, a lack of investment and careful consideration, or the struggle organizations have with implementing successful plans and procedures for SharePoint's restoration in the advent of a disaster.

So you can imagine my excitement and almost immediate satisfaction on reading the excellent business and technical guidance in this book. The fear and worry that had been bothering me, my customers, and my partners for so long became something we could understand, and more importantly, plan for by leveraging what we learned and what other people can learn from this book.

As a trusted advisor to many CIOs struggling with this very subject, and as a Microsoft Technology Strategist, I found this book to be great at spelling out the specific steps customers and partners would need to execute to achieve a successful disaster recovery strategy for SharePoint.

At times, the authors' observations and advice are thought-provoking and hit home for technology leaders tasked with ensuring that stakeholders understand the complexity and the reason why certain disaster recovery investments are needed. The technical guidance becomes invaluable as you begin to implement those same strategies within your own organization, or for a customer. Once assumptions have been replaced with facts, and as the complexities become clearer, you end up with a direction on how to move forward, and are ready to answer that dreaded question—how do we get SharePoint back up and running?

From experience, SharePoint is a powerful platform, which can be your most challenging enterprise technology or the one that keeps you up at night if not looked at with proper diligence and thought. The more powerful the platform is, the more ways it is leveraged, and the more critical it becomes. So don't hesitate testing your knowledge of SharePoint Disaster and Recovery after reading this book. Help ensure that your organization's significant investment of effort into SharePoint isn't lost, all because appropriate time, expertise, or money couldn't be found in your own organization.

Richard Harbridge

Partner Technology Strategist Microsoft

About the Authors

Peter Ward has worked with collaboration technology for over 20 years and is the founder of Soho Dragon Solutions, a New York based SharePoint consultancy. He has worked with some of the largest and most profitable companies in the USA, but also with the small ones that he calls the "Fortune 5,000,000". This is his fourth co-authored SharePoint book, the other three being *Microsoft SharePoint 2010 End User Guide: Business Performance Enhancement*, *Workflow in SharePoint 2010: Real World Business Workflow Solutions*, and *Microsoft SharePoint for Business Executives: Q&A Handbook*.

He has been a software guy forever, but is not much of a gadgeteer. In fact, he's probably a late adopter. He teaches yoga part-time in NYC and likes to serve up the perfect vegetarian dish.

> I would like to thank my wife, Peggy, for being the unofficial editor of the book. Even though she uses Lotus Notes at work and her company is the most anti-Microsoft company out there. I would also like to extend my appreciation to Shawn Conklin, Andrew Gregar, Julian Stevens, Willy Eyzaguirre, Kelly Meyer, and Jesse Wimberley, the book's chapter reviewers

Peter Abreu is an Enterprise, SharePoint, and Cloud Architect, with extensive experience architecting SharePoint 2007, 2010, and 2013 solutions on the cloud or on premises.

He is a frequent speaker at user groups, and has just done an all-day session at the SharePoint Best Practice Conference in DC. He was also a contributing author on the new *Microsoft SharePoint 2010 Administrators Companion* book for Microsoft Press.

In his spare time, he enjoys studying for new certifications, learning new technologies, and most of all spending time with his family. He lives in the Washington D.C metro area.

I would like to thank my wife, Mercedes, and my son, Sebastian, for their patience and support while I worked on this book. I would also like to thank my in-laws, Rogelio and America, as they supported me and pushed me to keep going when I first started studying SharePoint.

Pavlo Andrushkiw has spent nearly a decade in the Microsoft space delivering complex infrastructure solutions to a plethora of clients in various verticals. He currently works as the chief cloud architect for a major cloud services provider, migrating and deploying complex production environments for enterprise clients into the Amazon Web Services (AWS) infrastructure. This is his second co-authored SharePoint book, the first being *Microsoft SharePoint for Business Executives: Q&A Handbook*.

A special thanks to God, through whom all things are possible; to my parents for encouragement in all endeavors; to my lovely wife, pregnant with our second, for unyielding patience and support, and to my unborn child who can't believe the rate at which AWS releases new features and services.

Pat Esposito is the founder and CEO of IMPACT Management, a Microsoft partner based in Long Island, New York.

He has been working with SharePoint technologies since the initial 2001 release. Together with his partners, IMPACT aim's to "just make SharePoint easy". In his spare time, he enjoys spending time with his family, searching for the ultimate inexpensive wine or just cruising on his Harley Davidson.

I would like to thank my beautiful wife Eileen, without her commitment and endless love I would be totally lost; to my children Christina, Laura, and Nicholas who allow me to keep living vicariously; and our newest family member, our great dane Madeline who provides endless hours of amusement and distraction even when I don't want it.

Jeff Gellman is a Microsoft Certified IT Professional (MCITP) in Microsoft SharePoint and has over 12 years of experience with SharePoint going all the way back to the days of Tahoe. He has worked in all aspects of SharePoint projects including architecture, development, branding, infrastructure, disaster recovery, governance, backup and restore, migration and upgrade, and various third-party tools and utilities. With over 25 years of IT consulting experience, he has been involved in many projects over the years, for companies of all sizes, in roles ranging from developer to project manager with many of these projects having a heavy concentration on Microsoft technologies. He is a member of the Microsoft Virtual Technology Specialist Program (VTSP) and is a frequent speaker at events such as SharePoint Saturday.

In his spare time Jeff enjoys photography, listening to music, going to concerts, and watching and going to sporting events.

I would thank my wife, Danielle, for supporting me and encouraging me to take on new challenges such as working on this book. I would also like to thank my children, Jarrett and Samii, and step-daughters, Sarah and Hannah, for supporting me and giving me the quiet time I needed to work on this book.

Joel Plaut is a SharePoint consultant working with SharePoint since the SP2001 in a wide range of enterprises, with a focus on everything SharePoint, including MS-Project Server. His solutions encompass a range of technologies and disciplines, including PowerShell, .NET, Event Receivers, CAML, SQL, XSLT, XML, XPath, Web Services, C#, InfoPath, Workflows, SharePoint Designer but more importantly real world solutions to Document Management, Records Management, Migration to SharePoint, Upgrades, Content Management, Business Processes, Records Management, Search, Enterprise Taxonomy using Managed metadata Services, Content Syndication, and Portals.

His recent efforts include Excel Services, Business Connectivity Services, Managed Metadata Services, Business Intelligence, and wrestling diverse and chaotic farms into a modicum of structure with the gentle and appropriate application of governance and rational design based on applied Information Architecture.

He is a guitarist, skier, and all around MacGyver known for improvising a fix for almost anything with what is at hand, whether a toothpick or a French fry.

I would like to acknowledge my wife, Roz, for her incredible organization, and my kids Samantha, Heather, Lizzy, and Joshie for their reluctant acceptance of a technology nerd for a father.

About the Reviewers

Stefan Goßner works for Microsoft as a Senior Escalation Engineer in Microsoft Global Business Support. He provides third-level support for SharePoint products and technologies and Microsoft Content Management Server to customers. In this role he works directly with the product group to address customer problems through the development team if required.

He provides SharePoint related information on his personal blog: `http://blogs.technet.com/b/stefan_gossner`. The information he shares on his blog and his contribution in SharePoint forums have helped many customers around the globe to implement and maintain stable SharePoint environments.

He has co-authored the books *Building Websites With Microsoft Content Management Server* (ISBN 1-904811-16-7, Packt Publishing), *Advanced Microsoft Content Management Server Development* (ISBN 1-904811-53-1, Packt Publishing), and *Enhancing Microsoft Content Management Server with ASP.NET 2.0* (ISBN 1-904811-52-3, Packt Publishing) as well as several whitepapers around SharePoint.

He lives in Munich, Germany.

Sothilingam Jeyashanker is a Senior Consultant with NCS Pte Ltd. He enjoys solution design, administration, and development on the Microsoft SharePoint Products and Technologies platform. He has worked for many Microsoft Gold Partner companies as a consultant in the past years in Singapore. He obtained his Masters degree in Computer Science and Engineering from Anna University, Chennai, India.

I take this opportunity to thank three people. First is to The Government of Singapore for the opportunities provided by them for me to grow professionally as well as personally in this high-tech nation. Second is to my well-wisher/mentor, Mr Kamaludeen Mohamed Faizal (MVP), for his valuable time and advice. Third is to my Project Manager, Mr. Hamdan Othman, for his guidance and the extended help during my tough times during the project at NCS Pte Ltd.

Michael Nemtsev is a Senior Consultant working at Microsoft, helping clients to improve business productivity and collaboration using Office365, SharePoint, and Azure.

Doug Ortiz is an independent consultant whose skillset encompasses multiple platforms, such as .Net, SharePoint, Office, and SQL Server.

He possesses a Master's degree in Relational Databases and has over 20 years of experience in Information Technology. Of those years half have been within .NET and SharePoint. His roles have ranged from Architecture, Implementation, Administration, Disaster Recovery, Migrations, Development and Automation of Information Systems; in and outside of SharePoint.

He is the founder of Illustris, LLC and can be reached at dougortiz@illustris.org. He has experience in integrating multiple platforms and products with the purpose of sharing data, and has improved, salvaged, and architected projects by utilizing unique and innovative techniques.

His hobbies include Yoga and Scuba diving.

I would like to thank my wonderful wife, Mila, for all her help and support as well as Maria, Nikolay, and our wonderful children.

I would also like to thank everyone at Packt Publishing for their encouragement and guidance.

Richard Paterson is co-founder and Director of the international Microsoft Partner BrightStarr, specializing in SharePoint, Cloud, and Apps. He provides technical and architectural leadership to a team of consultants, architects, and software developers. He has been designing and developing for the web since its inception, and is passionate about its application in the business environment.

Prior to founding BrightStarr, he worked as an architect and developer in a broad range of industries, including weapons modeling and psychometric profiling.

In 2009, he was selected as one of the United Kingdom's top 30 young entrepreneurs in recognition of the rapid international growth of BrightStarr.

He has an Honors degree in Physics and is Microsoft accredited. Outside of work, he is a committed family man and an enthusiastic triathlete.

Daniele Proietti is a Microsoft-certified SharePoint architect and trainer with more than 20 years of experience in design and development of software. He has been working with SharePoint since version 2003.

He has a strong background in .NET, SQL Server, BizTalk, PowerBuilder, and Sybase.

He has worked on important projects for telecommunications, banking, insurance, public administration, financial police, utilities, and industry as technical specialist, team leader, and technical account manager.

He maintains a technical blog at `http://blogs.ugidotnet.org/dproietti`.

His LinkedIn profile is `http://www.linkedin.com/in/danieleproietti`.

Mikhail Pushin is an independent SharePoint Consultant who came into SharePoint world from the open source world. He has good expertise in both SharePoint administration and development fields.

He is an active member of the SharePoint community, and the majority of his answers (more than 300 per quarter) are marked as helpful and as solutions on Microsoft and Stack Exchange Forums.

He has widespread experience in SharePoint development; however, his favorite field is the new 2013 Workflow platform where he has very good insight. He shares this knowledge on his blog at `http://sp2013.pro`, where he publishes useful information and solutions, based on his experience in SharePoint world.

I'd like to thank my parents, Sergey and Lyubov, and my brother, Andrey, for teaching me to be the person I am today. I also want to thank my wife, Olga, and our son, Danil, for putting up with the extra hours spent reviewing this book.

www.PacktPub.com

Support files, eBooks, discount offers and more

You might want to visit www.PacktPub.com for support files and downloads related to your book.

Did you know that Packt offers eBook versions of every book published, with PDF and ePub files available? You can upgrade to the eBook version at www.PacktPub.com and as a print book customer, you are entitled to a discount on the eBook copy. Get in touch with us at service@packtpub.com for more details.

At www.PacktPub.com, you can also read a collection of free technical articles, sign up for a range of free newsletters and receive exclusive discounts and offers on Packt books and eBooks.

http://PacktLib.PacktPub.com

Do you need instant solutions to your IT questions? PacktLib is Packt's online digital book library. Here, you can access, read and search across Packt's entire library of books.

Why Subscribe?

- Fully searchable across every book published by Packt
- Copy and paste, print, and bookmark content
- On demand and accessible via web browser

Free Access for Packt account holders

If you have an account with Packt at www.PacktPub.com, you can use this to access PacktLib today and view nine entirely free books. Simply use your login credentials for immediate access.

Instant Updates on New Packt Books

Get notified! Find out when new books are published by following @PacktEnterprise on Twitter, or the *Packt Enterprise* Facebook page.

Table of Contents

Preface

The name of the game in this SharePoint book is SharePoint Disaster Recovery (DR), which also falls into the category of business continuity or high availability. The depth and breadth of the SharePoint DR can be quite daunting because often the reader is new to SharePoint and does not quite know how the pieces of the puzzle all fit together and is facing the challenge of determining how to implement a DR within their organization.

This book is structured to fill in the SharePoint knowledge gaps of how to apply a SharePoint DR approach that is documented, easy to understand, and is executable.

By applying knowledge from each chapter, this book will demystify the DR process and you will learn how to identify risk and appropriate DR approaches, and how to identify out-of-the-box SharePoint tools for your DR plans.

Why this book

Many organizations now use Microsoft's SharePoint platform for mission-critical applications, and business operations just cannot run without complete uptime of this technology. DR is the talking point for the IT department; it is one of the most important topics when it comes to SharePoint. Yet support of and an appropriate approach to this technology are still complex and often vulnerable to technical and business oversight and assumptions. This is stated in the Appendix section of the book.

This book provides a starting point to a complex subject, by offering clear and concise DR plans for the administrators to act upon.

Furthermore, it covers the key concepts and activities necessary to develop a disaster recovery plan for SharePoint. After covering these concepts, it dives into all of the crucial technical aspects of preserving SharePoint using Microsoft toolset.

 The most pertinent part of DR for any technology—not just SharePoint is to—remember where you left your installation disks and software keys!

This book outlines a few more steps than this.

How to start

Apart from taking note of the whereabouts of the installation disks and software keys, it is good practice for any organization to establish a Board or Governing Body to demonstrate a clear commitment to establishing and maintaining an effective DR planning process for SharePoint. This should be included with the other technologies, such as Exchange, SQL Server, and the network drive.

All management and staff should be informed that a disaster recovery plan is required in order to ensure essential functions of the organization are able to continue in the event of seriously adverse circumstances.

Once the full backing of the organization is obtained, the person or team developing the plan needs to prepare a workable approach. A good start is to create a list of all necessary documents and information. Where this includes documents containing sensitive information, care must be taken to ensure that confidentiality is not compromised.

Ranking key business areas

The DR plan should include a descriptive list of the organization's major business areas that are using SharePoint and for what purposes. This list should rank the business areas in order of importance to the overall organization. This is important because it allows prioritization of the recovery process, given that budget and resources are not infinite.

 You are dead in the water if Active Directory is not operational.

Each item should include a brief description of the business processes , as well as their dependencies on systems, communications, personnel, and information/data.

How to use this book

Our advice is simple: read the book from cover to cover. It should be a quick read. Make notes of the functions and your familiar process takeaways, and use post-it notes to label important techniques to which you want to refer. In fact, mark it up with a pen and think about how to apply the questions raised to technical staff, where to do some further research on a topic, and what discuss with other co-workers and team members to share and exchange ideas.

This book is designed to be a primer on the SharePoint DR technology and how to plan, document, and execute it, but not designed to be an endpoint to your SharePoint DR learning process.

What this book covers

Chapter 1, Planning and Key Concepts – What Not to Forget, is an introduction to SharePoint DR, how to approach the subject, and key concepts related to the subject. In this chapter, we will learn to identify the Disaster Recovery (DR) scenarios within SharePoint and its associated technology stack. It also covers inheriting a mission-critical environment that has no existing DR plans. It will highlight the traditional disaster recovery problem: the battle between cost and speed. It will enable us to think in terms of service disruptions versus disasters.

Chapter 2, Creating, Testing, and Maintaining the DR plan, explains how to test and maintain a SharePoint environment, so that the administrator has the ability to confidently say there is a solid DR plan in place. It explains how to identify all of the components and threats of your SharePoint environment. It includes a detailed explanations of how to create, test, and maintain your Disaster Recovery plan.

Chapter 3, Physical Backup and Restore Procedures, covers the backup and restore procedures for an on-premise environment that are available to an administrator, and explains their pros and cons. What is instrumental about this chapter is that it makes you think about what approach is appropriate to your individual implementation. This chapter discusses system state data backup, the partitioning of data, and the loss of data in Windows Server 2012. It also covers system database backups and restores, third-party database backups and restores, and point-in-time backups and restores.

Chapter 4, Virtual Environment Backup and Restore Procedures, covers backup and restore options for a virtual environment that are available to an administrator, and explains their pros and cons. What is instrumental about this chapter is that it makes you think about what approach is appropriate to your individual implementation. The topics covered in this chapter are Hyper V and VMware, backup and restore, Snapshots, and Failover clustering.

Chapter 5, Central Administration and Other Native Backup and Restore Options, lists the out-of-the-box SharePoint backup and restore methods, and their pros and cons. In this chapter, we will learn how to perform farm recovery by using a farm backup created with built-in tools. This chapter also explains component recovery using the farm backup system. It also highlights data recovery from an unattached content database and site collection recovery from a site collection backup.

Chapter 6, Working with Data Sizing and Data Structure, introduces you to the impact that data sizes may have no recovering SharePoint data and structure. This chapter will help you understand the data sizing architectural choices within a SharePoint environment. It explains how to work with very large amounts of data for recovery purposes. It also explains how to architect a SharePoint topology with Disaster Recovery in mind.

Chapter 7, Disaster Recovery with Custom Development, explains how to implement a solid DR strategy for custom development environments. In this chapter, you will become familiar with SharePoint development and understand its challenges. It also shows the steps needed to provide a recovery plan for customizations.

Chapter 8, Disaster Recovery Techniques for End Users, lists a number of recipes that the end user can introduce to their SharePoint activity in order to protect their own data. This chapter highlights points such as why training is often forgotten, some useful end user DR practices, managing expectations, and training.

Chapter 9, In the Clouds, demonstrates that SharePoint in the cloud is the talk of the town for most CIOs/CTOs, but the topic of conversation is normally security of data, rather than DR. This is partly because the media focuses on data security breaches, rather than site availability. Cloud DR is an important topic and should not be overlooked.

Chapter 10, Where to Start, wraps up the topics in the book and attempts to give the knowledge obtained from the book some sticking power to the reader.

The *Appendix* includes some horror stories of what went wrong and what should have been done, how and why assumptions can sink a DR plan, and best practices to keep a plan operational.

What you need for this book

For this book to be of value, you will need an open mind to absorb and interpret the advice and experience of the authors with regard the SharePoint topics that each chapter addresses. This is the key, because the book's emphasis is on planning, managing, and supporting SharePoint DR rather than proactive survival using step-by-step technical tasks.

You will also need the ability to reapply information given in the chapter topics to your deployed SharePoint environment. This information is not always going to be 100 percent relevant to how your organization works with the SharePoint technology, so not everything should be taken literally. The authors view this information as a guide to what the reader needs to do, and not as the truth itself. To become experienced with DR you must experience the truth, not just blindly accept what you read.

Who this book is for

This book is ideal for SharePoint administrators who want to sleep at night in the comfort of knowing that their SharePoint environment is recoverable so that it can support Line Of Business (LOB) activities in the event of a disaster. It explains the SharePoint DR in bite-size chunks and at a technical level, yet arms you with enough knowledge to make DR decisions, ask further questions to your technical teams, and make necessary DR-related decisions.

This book is not designed for the developer or CIO, although the content may be of interest in providing a common vocabulary and vision between the developers, the CIO, and the administrators.

Conventions

In this book, you will find a number of styles of text that distinguish between different kinds of information. Here are some examples of these styles, and an explanation of their meaning.

Code words in text are shown as follows: "To get a list of available services, you can use the `Get-SPServiceInstance` cmdlet".

A block of code is set as follows:

```
$webapp = Get-SPwebapplication "http://SharePoint"
$webapp | get-spsite -Limit ALL | ForEach-Object {
  $site = $_;
  $site;
  $site.quota;
}
$site.dispose()
$webapp.dispose()
```

Any command-line input or output is presented as follows:

```
$TJ.set_DaysToKeepHistory(3)
$TJ.update()
```

New terms and **important words** are shown in bold. Words that you see on the screen, in menus or dialog boxes for example, appear in the text like this: "In the **Actions** pane, click on **Backup Once**."

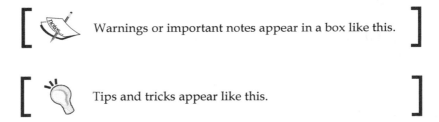

Warnings or important notes appear in a box like this.

Tips and tricks appear like this.

Reader feedback

Feedback from our readers is always welcome. Let us know what you think about this book—what you liked or may have disliked. Reader feedback is important for us to develop titles that you really get the most out of.

To send us general feedback, simply send an e-mail to feedback@packtpub.com, and mention the book title in the subject of your message.

If there is a book that you need and would like to see us publish, please send us a note via the **SUGGEST A TITLE** form on www.packtpub.com, or e-mail suggest@packtpub.com.

If there is a topic that you have expertise in and on which you are interested in either writing or contributing to a book, see our author guide on www.packtpub.com/authors.

Customer support

Now that you are the proud owner of a Packt book, we have a number of things to help you to get the most from your purchase.

Errata

Although we have taken every care to ensure the accuracy of our content, mistakes do happen. If you find a mistake in one of our books — maybe a mistake in the text or the code — we would be grateful if you would report this to us. By doing so, you can save other readers from frustration and help us improve subsequent versions of this book. If you find any errata, please report them by visiting http://www.packtpub. com/support, selecting your book, clicking on the **errata submission form** link, and entering the details of your errata. Once your errata are verified, your submission will be accepted and the errata will be uploaded on our website, or added to any list of existing errata, under the Errata section of that title. Any existing errata can be viewed by selecting your title from http://www.packtpub.com/support.

Piracy

Piracy of copyright material on the Internet is an ongoing problem across all media. At Packt, we take the protection of our copyright and licenses very seriously. If you come across any illegal copies of our works, in any form, on the Internet, please provide us with the location address or website name immediately so that we can pursue a remedy.

Please contact us at copyright@packtpub.com with a link to the suspected pirated material.

We appreciate your help in protecting our authors, and our ability to bring you valuable content.

Questions

You can contact us at questions@packtpub.com if you are having a problem with any aspect of the book, and we will do our best to address it.

Planning and Key Concepts – What Not to Forget

The purpose of this chapter is to establish a foundation for the reader, by identifying the key concepts, both technical and operational, that will eventually need to be applied to a SharePoint deployment within an organization.

In this chapter, we will cover:

- Identifying **Disaster Recovery** (**DR**) scenarios within SharePoint and its associated technology stack
- Inheriting a mission critical environment that has no existing DR plans
- Traditional DR – the battle between cost and speed
- Thinking in terms of service disruptions versus disasters
- Four datacenter outages in 2012 that we can learn from
- Building confidence by refining DR plans with more frequent testing
- What is virtualization and how does it help with DR?
- Efficiently supporting hybrid environments with virtualized DR
- Cloud based solutions welcoming a new approach

Identifying DR scenarios within SharePoint and its associated technology stack

Tackling DR in a SharePoint environment is often a struggle for both seasoned SharePoint administrators and newbies, because of the different ways in which the platform can be deployed within an organization. Furthermore, it can prove to be challenging to apply existing DR experience to SharePoint, due to the distributed and componentized nature of SharePoint and the supporting technologies that need to be in place for SharePoint to function. SharePoint relies on technologies such as Microsoft SQL Server, **Active Directory Domain Services (ADDS)**, **Internet Information Services (IIS)**, and .NET framework just to name a few, so there are a lot of dependencies and points of failure to identify during the DR planning stage.

 It is not enough to think it is being backed up so we can restore it easily. It is more, what has failed and what parts need to be restored to be operational again.

Why disasters happen and what you can do to prevent them?

In IT there is a misconception that more documentation, procedures, and processes, equals better documentation, procedures, and processes. The fact is that the opposite is true. The first thing that you should implement to avoid tons of documentation, procedures, and processes that may be redundant or contradictory is to, as per best practice; create a solid governance plan that details your procedures and processes.

A good governance plan is a living document that requires constant revision and adjustment to maintain a crisp and agile process. The administrators who do the work should own the processes and maintain them with the help and input of the business stakeholders. I have seen too many businesses where the stakeholders define the policies and procedures thinking only about the business needs and giving little or no thought to the technical side of things, so the documentation and procedures are unrealistic and prone to failure.

Success or failure

SharePoint environments are extremely complex systems that require constant monitoring, planning, and maintenance; you cannot just deploy a farm and hope to have a stable, secure collaboration platform. This is why having a solid and well thought out governance plan is crucial. But the reality is that most organizations either don't have a proper governance plan or don't have one at all.

One of the main causes of system failure is when processes and procedures are weak, this usually happens when the people who are responsible for creating, implementing, and tweaking the processes and procedures (usually the governance board) are not monitoring and reviewing the processes and procedures continually to keep them up-to-date, and the administrators are not testing on a regular basis and reporting back to the governance board informing them of the issues that were found with the processes and procedures while testing. So what usually happens is that the administrators start coming up with quick fixes and workarounds to keep things going in the short term but sooner or later, they will get tired, frustrated, or they'll leave before things really go wrong. Then, it is too late to prevent the catastrophe that has been brewing.

So management must understand that they need enough staff on the ground not just to keep things up and running but to maintain a healthy and stable environment, they need to have a well thought out governance plan. Staff on the ground must report situations that will lead to system failure and data loss to management immediately.

Is failure necessary for success? I think that processes and procedures must be tested and improved continuously, testing is how you will find weaknesses and flaws in your processes and procedures that you may not find in the midst of a system failure. This is the main reason for governance, people taking ownership of change and reacting to it constructively. So the answer is yes, failure is necessary for success, but if you are testing regularly these failures will happen in a controlled environment.

Inheriting a mission critical environment that has no DR plans

A part of the problem for an administrator is to understand how the supporting technology stack integrates with SharePoint. Although an administrator may know ADDS, IIS, and SQL Server, and how these software stacks work, they may be unfamiliar as to how these technologies work together with SharePoint. This topic is covered in later chapters of this book.

The other challenge with SharePoint DR is that an administrator may not realize or understand the business activity that is reliant on SharePoint, and will have a hard time putting together an appropriate DR plan. With e-mail, there is no question that this is considered mission critical and needs constant uptime in an organization. But with SharePoint, this may not always be the case.

 Perish the thought. Someone in IT needs to wear a business hat and speak to the business managers, understand their business needs and SharePoint activities, and how mission critical these are. This should not be a once a year exercise, but rather an ongoing interaction so that the entire team is on the same page and completely understands the business needs.

Worst case – loss of SharePoint environment without proper backups

In scenarios where proper backups were not done, restoring a SharePoint server is much more problematic. Because SharePoint does not run in a vacuum, proper planning must account for three components: SQL, IIS, and Active Directory.

SQL-specific issues will be covered later in this chapter. In regards to server restoration, remember that if a SQL alias was not used, SQL may not perform as expected when renamed. Although most connections to a SQL Server are socket or named pipe-based, a rename can cause some aberrant behavior if not properly planned. In addition to this issue, permissions at the instance and database level also merit inspection.

For more information see Plan for backup and recovery in SharePoint 2013 available at:

`http://technet.microsoft.com/en-us/library/cc261687.aspx`

For more information see Backup and restore: SharePoint server 2013 available at:

`http://www.microsoft.com/en-us/download/details.aspx?id=30365`

IIS maintains configuration in the Metabase. Its location and tools for management changed between IIS 6.0 (server 2003) and IIS 7.0 (server 2008). In the early versions of IIS, the web server's configuration was stored in an XML file.

Under the current versions of IIS, the configuration is saved in the application's `host.config` or `web.config` files. Previously, backup and restoration of this data was integrated into the IIS Manager utility. The command line tool `appcmd` is used for disaster protection of the configuration.

The `AppCmd.exe` file is located in the `%systemroot%\system32\inetsrv\` directory. This is not the path so it will not start automatically; you need to use the full path to the executable when executing commands, that is, `%systemroot%\system32\inetsrv\AppCmd.exe` list sites or you can manually add the `inetsrv` directory to the path on your machine so that you can access the `AppCmd.exe` file directly from any location. Data in the Metabase is specific to the current web applications and settings and may be lost if simply moving a site to a different server.

Active Directory is another service that touches SharePoint in several ways. The primary concern is ensuring that the computer account for the SharePoint server has the correct memberships in Active Directory. The various service accounts and permission groups for SharePoint are also held in Active Directory. If the identity of the server was maintained, then Active Directory will not need to change when the server is restored. Otherwise, remapping the old identity to the new one may be necessary.

Disaster protection of a SharePoint server is a layered approach. The outer ring of software protection is the operating system. Protection and restoration of the operating system is the first and a critical step in restoring a SharePoint server. The most important goal in server restoration is maintaining the identity of the server, even in cases where both the software and hardware are destroyed. The second step is to identify the factor that shapes and, in many cases, dictates a restoration strategy. A proper DR plan will allow rapid restoration of the server, sometimes with several options available.

Disaster Recovery – cost versus speed

When choosing a DR approach, organizations rely on the level of service required, as measured by two recovery objectives:

- **Recovery time objective (RTO)**: This is the amount of time between an outage and the restoration of operations

- **Recovery point objective (RPO)**: This is the point in time where data is restored and it reflects the amount of data that will be ultimately lost during the recovery process

The preceding objectives are still relevant with SharePoint and the amount of money the business is willing to spend. This is covered in depth in *Chapter 2, Creating, Testing, and Maintaining the DR Plan*, and *Chapter 6, Working with Data Sizing and Data Structure*.

With dedicated and shared DR models, organizations are often forced to make trade-offs between cost and speed. As the necessity to achieve high availability and reduce costs continues to increase, organizations can no longer accept trade-offs, that is, a bank, for example, cannot use a cold standby model because it's cheaper, the C-level executives, that is, your CIO is going to want to know why it took 4 or 5 days to recover and why was there loss of data costing your organization possibly thousands of dollars. There is no set rule for this, except how much is your organization willing to pay and how much data loss is acceptable that is the formula.

Most organizations where SharePoint is mission critical use a hot standby; this is a duplicate farm in a DR datacentre. Depending on how much downtime is acceptable to your organization and how much time you want to spend on maintaining both farms synchronized, you would make the following decisions:

- Just have three servers running and the rest turned off, and in the case of a disaster you would turn on the rest of the servers, and add whatever solutions and patches need to be added.

- Have all your servers live all the time; this is much faster but obviously more expensive

- Have all your servers live all the time and use a third-party tool, such as **Metalogix Replicator** (C) for real time synchronization

I was the lead architect for `recovery.gov`. They have 45 servers on the AWS cloud in one region and 45 servers in their DR region. Although all the servers are live, it is not an active active environment; it is an active passive environment.

In case of a disaster, they would need to fail over to their DR farm manually, this is about a 1 hour window that is expectable to them. So you see the decision is yours; what is an acceptable loss of data and what is an acceptable amount of down-time?

While DR was originally intended for critical back-office processes, many organizations are now dependent on real-time enterprise applications like SharePoint that handle everything from their internet, intranet and extranet which are primary interfaces for their clients and employees. The cost of a minute of downtime may cost them thousands of dollars.

Standby datacentres are required for scenarios where local redundant systems and backups cannot recover from the outage at the primary datacentre. The time to get a farm up and running in a different location is often known as a hot, warm, or cold standby. Our definitions for these farm recovery datacentres are as follows:

- **Cold standby**: A redundancy method that involves having one system as a backup for another identical primary system that can provide availability within hours or days.
- **Warm standby**: A redundancy method that involves having one system running in the background of an identical primary system that can provide availability within minutes or hours.
- **Hot standby**: A redundant method of having one system running simultaneously with another identical primary system that can provide availability within seconds or minutes.

Each of these standby datacentres have an associated cost to operate and maintain.

- **Cold standby DR strategy**: A business ships backups to an offsite storage site regularly, and has contracts in place for emergency server rentals.

  Pros:

  ◦ The cheapest option to maintain, operationally.

  Cons:

  ◦ The slowest option to recover.
  ◦ Often an expensive option to recover, because it requires that physical servers be configured correctly after a disaster has occurred.
  ◦ Some datacentres do not have the SharePoint expertise in house to deploy and configure your farm, so you will need to implement a solution to facilitate this, such as Microsoft's **System Center Data Protection Manager** or PowerShell script. You may still run into problems such as the hardware not being the same, this can cause all sorts of problems and delays.

- **Warm standby DR strategy**: A business ships/uploads backups or virtual machine images to local and regional disaster recovery farms.

  Pros:

  ○ Often fairly inexpensive to recover, because a virtual server farm can require little configuration upon recovery.

  Cons:

  ○ Can be very expensive and time consuming to maintain.

  ○ You pay lots of money in storage fees, that is, if you take a backup of one of your servers and it is 90 GB in size, the virtual machine will be 90 GB in size; multiply that by 6 or 10 servers and the cost of uploading that data every time you send the datacentre a new backup not to mention the cost of having them upload those images and of course test them at least once a month. (Remember: if you haven't tested it and had a successful restore it is not a good DR plan it's a shot in the dark.)

- **Hot standby DR strategy**: A business runs multiple datacentres, but serves content and services through only one datacentre.

  Pros:

  ○ It is often fairly fast to recover. If you are using third-party tools, such as Metalogix Replicator (C), that can synchronize two or more distant SharePoint farms in real time you can ensure that SharePoint content is always available and up-to-date. Bi-directional replication syncs all your SharePoint content; documents, sites, applications, permissions, and workflows with full metadata, versioning, and permissions. Replicator can sync immediately after changes happen or on a regular schedule.

  Cons:

  ○ Can be very expensive to configure and maintain, that is, you have to add the cost of all the Microsoft licensing and third party tools like Replicator.

 It does not matter which of the preceding DR solutions you decide to implement, there will probably be some data loss, as seen in the following examples unless you are using third-party tools, such as Metalogix Replicator.

Cold standby recovery

In a cold standby disaster recovery scenario, you have to recover by setting up a new farm in your cold standby datacentre and restore the backups that you have stored there. In this scenario, if your primary farm fails before you get to make the backups to ship out to the cold standby datacentre, you will lose all the data added or changed since your last backup.

Warm standby recovery

In a warm standby disaster recovery scenario, you have to create a duplicate farm in the warm standby datacentre and ensure that it is updated regularly by using full and incremental backups of the farm in the primary datacentre. This requires some continuous monitoring, server maintenance, SharePoint upgrades, and other data activity to keep the environment warm. In the event of a failure, you will lose all the data added or changed since your last backup.

Virtual warm standby environments

Virtualization provides a cost effective option for a warm standby recovery solution. Typically, you can use Hyper-V or VMware as an in-house solution for recovery. This is explained in further detail in *Chapter 4, Virtual Environment Backup and Restore Procedures*. But even this has its downside. If it takes two days for the VMs or backups to get to the DR datacentre or to upload all the VMs to the DR datacenter, your backups are now two days out of date.

Otherwise, you have to make sure that the virtual images are created often enough to provide the level of farm configuration and content freshness that you must have for recovering the farm at the secondary DR site. You must have an environment available in which you can host the VMs. We will dig a bit deeper into virtualization technologies later in this chapter.

Hot standby recovery

In a hot standby disaster recovery scenario, you have to create a duplicate farm in the hot standby datacentre, so that it can assume production operations almost immediately after the primary farm fails. This requires a third-party tool, such as Metalogix Replicator for real time synchronization.

For more information on Metalogix Replicator visit,
`http://www.metalogix.com/Products/Replicator/`
`Replicator-for-SharePoint.aspx`.

Both the RTO and RPO approaches include shared and dedicated models. These are explained below.

Dedicated model

In a dedicated model, the infrastructure is dedicated to a single organization. Compared to other traditional models, this can offer a faster time for recovery, because the IT infrastructure is mirrored at the disaster recovery site and is ready to be called upon in the event of a disaster. While this model can reduce RTO because the hardware and software are preconfigured, it does not eliminate all delays. You still need to restore the data. This approach is costly because the hardware sits idle when not being used for disaster recovery. Some organizations use the DR infrastructure for development and testing, to mitigate the cost, but that introduces additional risk. When organizations start using their DR site for development or test, it becomes a huge problem because when the time comes to use it for an actual disaster, the farms are not the same; they are drastically different. There are solutions that were not maintained or documented correctly and now you are in a bind.

 There are also SharePoint license costs to consider. Yes, you still have to have any servers that are receiving data fully licensed while they are idle.

Shared model

In a shared model, the infrastructure is shared among multiple organizations so it is more cost effective. After a disaster is declared, the hardware, the operating system, and the application software at the disaster site must be configured from the ground up to match the IT site that has declared a disaster. On top of that, the data restoration process must be completed. This can take hours or even days.

This is normally a service provided by the company that is managing your data operations.

Hybrid model

There is a hybrid model, where a certain SharePoint technology such as SQL Server leverages a DR process from another application; this does reduce costs, but of course both DR plans need to be in sync. This can also become very complex; how do you separate the two and when it comes to restoring what is the process? I personally don't like this model because of its complexity, and as a best practice it is never a good idea to add any other database to your SharePoint SQL Server.

Thinking of interruptions and not disasters

Most people think of disaster recovery as a plan that is in place in case of a disaster, such as:

- Weather related events, such as floods, tornadoes, hurricanes, and forest/brush fires
- Earthquakes

Any of these disasters can disable your primary datacentre and you would have to failover to your DR datacentre. However, most application interruptions are due to more mundane everyday occurrences, such as:

- Facility fires
- Fiber or communication lines are cut – loss of network
- Power failures – outage or sporadic service
- Cut power line
- Security breach – hacking and/or malicious code
- Water pipe breaks in a facility
- Human error, such as a redundant system's failure that goes unnoticed

These interruptions can cripple a business if the business does not have a proper DR plan in place.

Another dimension to this point is covered in *Chapter 8, Disaster Recovery Techniques for End Users*. Think of who is interrupted: sales force, trading floor, executives, or end users.
This may seem like a trivial point, but IT has only so much manpower to dedicate to issues.

Four major datacenter outages in 2012 that we can learn from

This prompted greater focus on architecting cloud-based applications across multiple zones and locations for greater resilience:

- **Super storm sandy, Oct 29-30**: Datacenters in New York and New Jersey were impacted by the storm ranging from downtime because of flooding to days on generator power for data centers around the region. Sandy was a storm that caused more than just a single outage, and tested the resilience and determination of the data center industry on an unprecedented scale.

- **Go Daddy DNS outage, Sept 10**: Go Daddy is one of the biggest DNS service providers, as it hosts 5 million websites and manages more than 50 million domain names. That's why the Sept 10 outage was one of the most disruptive incidents of 2012. The six-hour incident was a result of corrupted data in router tables.

- **Amazon Outage, June 29-30**: AWS EC2 cloud computing service powers some of the web's most popular sites and services, including Netflix, Heroku, Pinterest, Quora, Hootsuite and Instagram. A system of strong thunderstorms, known as a **derecho**, rolled through northern Virginia causing a power outage to the AWS Ashburn datacenter. The generators failed to operate properly, depleting the emergency power in the **Uninterruptible Power Supply (UPS)** systems.

- **Calgary data center fire, July 11**: A datacenter fire in the Shaw Communications facility in Calgary, Alberta delayed hundreds of surgeries at the local hospitals. The fire disabled both the primary and backup systems that supported key public services. This was a wake-up call for government agencies to ensure that the datacenters that manage emergency services have failover systems.

This is why having a well-planned DR strategy is so important, because of unforeseen assurances like the preceding ones.

What is virtualization and how does it help with DR?

When you think of virtualization, think of it as a way of consolidating servers. Virtualization is the process of separating the software layer of a server from its hardware layer. A new layer is placed between the two to act as a go-between this is known as the hypervisor.

Companies used to have multiple servers with each server operating system on its own piece of server hardware. In virtualization the server, including the operating system, applications, patches, and data, is encapsulated into a single image or virtual server.

A single physical server, called the host, can run four or five of these images or virtual servers simultaneously, saving the company money on the following:

- Purchase of hardware, as less servers are needed
- Consolidate management of the machines
- Reduced energy consumption, as there are less servers
- Much more efficient use of resources, as the new machine(s) will be able to share those resources
- Failure in one machine will not lead to the failure of others

Most computers operate using as little as 4 percent to 7 percent of their resources. There are many visualization companies in the market; the two that we have mentioned in this chapter are Microsoft Hyper-V and VMware.

How does virtualization help with DR?

In virtualization, the server, including the operating systems, applications, patches, and data is all encapsulated into a single virtual server, it improves redundancy as the virtual server can be restored on another host if needed.

Supporting mixed environments more efficiently with virtualized disaster recovery

As the complexity of IT departments increases, including multiple server farms, multiple farm environments, and federated farms, the ability to respond to a disaster or outage has become more complex. Depending on what standby recovery model you are using, you may need to recover on different hardware, which can take longer and increase the possibility for errors and data loss.

Organizations are implementing virtualization technologies, such as Hyper-V and VMware in their datacenters to help remove some of the underlying complexities, and optimize infrastructure utilization. Cloud-based business resilience solutions must offer both **Physical-to-Virtual (P2V)** and **Virtual-to-Virtual (V2V)** recovery, in order to support these types of environments.

What about the cloud?

Cloud computing refers to both the applications delivered as services over the Internet and the hardware and software systems in the datacenters that provide those services.

When a cloud is made available in a pay-as-you-go manner to the public, we call it a public cloud; the service being sold is **Utility Computing**. Current examples of public clouds include Amazon web services, Google, Rackspace, and Microsoft Azure.

The term 'private cloud' refers to internal datacenters of a business or other organization that are not made available to the public.

There are three major cloud models:

- **Software as a Service (SaaS)**: SalesForce, Microsoft 365
- **Platform as a Service (PaaS)**: MS Windows Azure
- **Infrastructure as a Service (IaaS)**: AWS, Rackspace, and most recently Azure came up with IaaS

Because the servers are on demand and do not need to be purchased, there are a lot of benefits with cloud computing. There is huge cost benefit, as well as rapid provisioning, scalability, and elasticity. Some cloud vendors even offer a complete DR package and can allow an outsourcing of your DR to them. The last chapter in this book is dedicated to evaluating DR in the context of the cloud.

Building confidence and refining DR plans with frequent testing

It is a good practice to test your DR plan regularly by failing over to your DR site. I would suggest doing this failover test once a month, but this may not be possible for all enterprises, at the very least, you should be doing it once a quarter to gain confidence and peace of mind knowing that you have a solid and reliable DR plan that works. You have no idea how many clients I have been to that tell me they have a solid DR plan but when we test it they rarely work! This mind-set exists because too many companies believe in set it and forget it, as we mentioned previously, you must test your DR by failing over to your DR site to ensure that it works.

You wouldn't want to find all the issues in your DR plan in the middle of a disaster. Backups alone are useless if you don't have a place to restore them. The way to go from ought to work to known to work is through testing!

The reasons for infrequent testing are usually budgets and the scarcity of time. This is why most failures are usually discovered during a disaster. And at that time you have a few or no practical alternatives.

A well-developed Disaster Recovery plan will identify all key processes and steps to failover to your DR site. It should have a predefined schedule for testing, after each test document any weakness found and what was done to correct them.

New technologies, such as virtualization and cloud computing make regular and (even daily) testing feasible. These technologies allow you to automate processes and provide a foundation for an ongoing RTO and RPO reporting at the management level, allowing you to better estimate and mitigate risks for the business.

Summary

This chapter has set the stage so that readers understand and are aware of the importance of planning and creating a SharePoint DR plan to support their SharePoint deployment.

The following chapter explain how to perform testing and maintenance on a DR environment so the administrator has the confidence that the documentation is actually workable.

2
Creating, Testing, and Maintaining the DR Plan

In the previous chapter, you were introduced to the planning concepts of DR and where to start with a DR plan. This chapter introduces you to the activities around creating, testing, and maintaining an effective DR plan for your SharePoint environment. Before creating a test plan, one must have a clear understanding of what each component of your SharePoint farm is, the role it plays, and the threats that each of these components face, that could necessitate the DR plan being exercised.

A SharePoint farm is a collection of SharePoint servers and SQL servers that work together to provide a set of basic SharePoint services that support a single website.

The ability of multiple servers is to work in conjunction and provide a system with its failover capabilities and load balancing. The servers can also provide readily-available backups that can scale to immense sizes. Useful for DR!

Within a farm, there are several services that run on one or more servers. These services provide basic functionality for SharePoint and regulate which services should run on which servers, in an effort to manage the impact of a failure on the overall farm architecture and performance.

There are occasions when multiple SharePoint farms make sense. An enterprise might have a **quality assurance** (**QA**) farm and a production farm. Geographically dispersed enterprises might have a farm in Europe, one in the Asia-Pacific region, and another in North America.

In this chapter, we will cover the following topics:

- How to identify the components of your SharePoint environment
- How to identify threats to your SharePoint environment
- How to create an effective DR plan
- How to test your DR plan
- How to maintain your DR plan

Getting started

Imagine you are the administrator of a SharePoint implementation for a large company that uses SharePoint for their corporate intranet, collaboration websites, enterprise search, and other mission-critical business processes. One day you are sitting at your desk and you get a call from a user saying that they are receiving an error when trying to access the intranet.

As you begin looking at this, you receive several more phone calls as well as e-mails from other users experiencing the same problem. You attempt to remotely log in to the SharePoint Central Administration server to check on the server logs and **Unified Logging System** (**ULS**) logs. However, there is no response from the server. What do you do now?

You begin with basic troubleshooting to see if you can determine what the issue is and to see if you can get it corrected in a timely manner. However, in this particular case you discover that your server, which runs Central Administration and several key SharePoint services, has died.

This would be the time to refer to your DR plan (ideally not saved in SharePoint) to see what to do next assuming you had a plan. Even if you had a plan, are you sure it will work? Has it been tested? These are the kind of questions that need to be answered before a disaster occurs, not after you are in the midst of one.

So how do you start with a SharePoint DR plan? There are some preliminary steps you should take as part of developing your SharePoint DR plan. These steps include identifying each component of your SharePoint environment and the threats to each component that could cause a disaster.

Identifying the components of your SharePoint environment

Before creating a DR plan, you should take a complete inventory of each component of your SharePoint environment. This inventory should include the following:

- The physical architecture, such as the servers, the database, and the network
- The logical architecture, such as web applications, service accounts, service applications, and apps
- Custom software installed in the farm

Physical architecture

You should begin the process of taking an inventory of each component of your SharePoint environment starting with the physical architecture. The physical architecture should include all farms and related components in your SharePoint environment, including any development, testing, staging, QA, and production farms.

Although the other SharePoint farms aside from your production farm may not be part of your SharePoint DR plan, it is good practice to make sure that you have an inventory of each farm. You may need to utilize individual components of the physical architecture of any of these environments as part of your overall SharePoint DR plan should you experience a failure in any of the physical components of your production SharePoint farm.

 As part of the process of identifying the physical architecture of your SharePoint farms, you should create easy-to-read diagrams using a tool similar to Microsoft Visio.

Servers

Each server in each SharePoint farm in your environment, needs to be identified. The information collected for each server should include the following:

- Server name
- Server description/purpose
- Server location
- Physical or virtual
- Host name (if virtual)
- **Internet Protocol (IP)** addresses:
    - Internal
    - External (if applicable)
- Operating System (including service packs, patch level and hotfixes)
- Processor(s)
- RAM
- **Network Interface Cards (NIC)**
- Hard drives:
    - Drive letter
    - Drive type (internal, **Storage Area Network (SAN)**)
    - Space
    - Purpose
- Backup schedule
- Services and roles:
    - Application server role
    - IIS
    - **Simple Mail Transport Protocol (SMTP)**
    - Others

- Installed software (version, service packs, patch level and hotfixes):
  - ° SharePoint
  - ° Anti-virus
  - ° Utilities
  - ° Tools
  - ° Others

Database

A complete inventory of all SharePoint related database servers should be collected. It may be necessary to work with a DBA to gather this information. Information gathered should include the following:

- SQL Server version (including service packs, patch level and hotfixes)
- SQL Server configuration (standalone, mirrored, clustered, always on, and so on)
- Database instances:
  - ° Names
- Databases:
  - ° Names
  - ° Data file name
  - ° Data file location
  - ° Log file name
  - ° Log file location
  - ° Settings (auto-growth, log file size, and so on)
- Additional Services (reporting services, analysis services, integration services, and so on)
- Backup Tools
- Backup schedule:
  - ° Full
  - ° Incremental

Network

In order to get as much detail as possible about your SharePoint environment and to help you to develop your SharePoint DR plan, you should include details about the network(s) used by the SharePoint environment. Information collected about your network should include the following:

- Network topology:
    - ° Internal
    - ° External (if applicable)
- **Domain Name Service (DNS)** mappings
- Load balancers (if applicable):
    - ° Virtual IP mappings
- Firewall rules

Logical architecture

The next step in the process of taking an inventory of each component of your SharePoint environment deals with the logical architecture. The logical architecture should include the high-level logical components in your SharePoint environment, including all development, testing, staging, QA, and production farms.

Web applications

The highest level in a SharePoint logical architecture for a SharePoint farm is the Web application. The information collected for each Web application in every one of your SharePoint farms should include the following:

- Web application name
- **Uniform Resource Locator (URL)**
- Port(s)
- Alternate access mappings
- Content database name(s)
- Application pool(s)
- Authentication provider(s)
- Additional settings
- `web.config` files
- IIS settings (that is, host headers)

Service accounts

It is important to identify each service account used by each SharePoint farm in the environment. Service account information that should be captured is as follows:

- Service account name
- Purpose
- Local rights
- Domain rights

Service applications

Each SharePoint farm will have several associated service applications. Service application information that should be captured is as follows:

- Service application name
- Service application description
- Server(s) running the service application
- Service application pool(s)
- Service application database name(s)
- Service application service account(s)
- Additional Settings (for example, the Secure Store Service application needs to record and keep the passphrase that is used to encrypt the credential, in a secure location)

Apps

SharePoint 2013 introduces the concept of the apps model to the product. Apps are essentially web applications that fit seamlessly into the SharePoint website where they are installed, and therefore bring data and functionality to the users' familiar work environment.

For example, let's say you have a SharePoint website that is used to collaborate with a team, and you want to create a survey to gather more data. In SharePoint 2013, you can get a survey app, from the Office Store or from your SharePoint app catalog, and install it on your website.

Apps can be hosted in a variety of different ways, including in a private cloud, a public cloud such as Windows Azure, or directly within SharePoint. The following diagram summarizes the critical aspects of the various hosting approaches for the SharePoint 2013 App model:

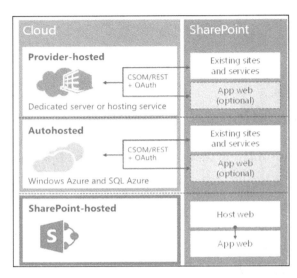

You should capture information about all of the apps that are installed and used in your SharePoint farm, so that if you need to recover your environment in the event of a disaster you can reconfigure all of the apps in the farm. Information that should be collected about SharePoint apps is as follows:

- App name
- App ID
- App description/purpose
- App domain
- App service settings
- App authentication configuration

 Additional information on DR the SharePoint apps can be found in *Chapter 7, Disaster Recovery with Custom Development*.

Identifying threats to your SharePoint environment

Now that you have an inventory of each of the components of your SharePoint environment, the next step is to identify threats to the key components that should be included in your SharePoint DR plan. The primary threats that could affect your SharePoint environment and put you in a DR situation are typically related to the physical architecture as opposed to the logical architecture. This section focuses on threats to your physical architecture, although you should be aware that threats to your logical architecture, such as issues with web applications, service applications, and apps could also affect your SharePoint environment and put you in DR situation.

Physical architecture

Any disruption or failure in the physical architecture of your SharePoint environment can cause downtime, which could necessitate activating the SharePoint DR plan, if the issue could not be resolved through normal troubleshooting. Such a situation could be a natural disaster, such as a flood, hurricane, or earthquake that would knock your primary datacenter offline.

The following sections identify the key components of the physical architecture, and the threats to each that should be considered in your SharePoint DR plan.

Servers

A SharePoint farm consists of any number of servers from a single-server farm to a large scale multi-server enterprise farm. A failure of any of these servers can have a dramatic effect on the farm, from degraded performance to complete failure. Typically, the biggest failure at the server level is hardware-related. Whether it is a bad NIC, a failed drive, a drive that's run out of space, or some other hardware issue, the failure of any one of these key components can cause downtime in your SharePoint farm and should therefore be accounted for in your DR plan.

It is recommended that ongoing monitoring and periodic testing of your hardware health can go a long way to prevent the kind of hardware failure that could cause a disaster in your SharePoint farm. Items that should be monitored and tested are as follows:

- CPUs
- Hard drives
- NIC(s)
- Memory

Database

The heart of any SharePoint implementation is the database. A failure at the database level would have a significant effect on the performance and/or availability of the related SharePoint farm. Failures that typically occur at the database level involve a drive failure (local or SAN), a corrupted database or transaction log file, a full transaction log, a hung database transaction, a hung database lock, or the SQL Server service has stopped running.

Database administrators should set up monitors and jobs to identify and eliminate issues that could pose a risk to the health of the database, which could cause a disaster in your SharePoint farm. Items that should be monitored are as follows:

- Drive space
- Log size
- Transactions
- Disk I/O
- Database locks

Network

If your SharePoint servers cannot communicate with each other, or cannot be reached by end users, this is a certain recipe for disaster. Preparing for a network failure, including a network hardware failure, including the failure of switches, routers, load balancers, or a network software failure, for example, failure of the DNS or Directory services, for example, Active Directory will be a key piece of your SharePoint DR plan.

Setting up monitoring of your network and key components of your network infrastructure can help in identifying potential disasters in your SharePoint environment before they occur. Items that should be monitored are as follows:

- Network latency
- Network speed
- Server load

 For more information, please navigate to the page titled "Plan for monitoring in SharePoint 2013" at http://technet.microsoft.com/en-us/library/jj219701.aspx.

Creating an effective DR plan

Now that you have an inventory of each of the components of your SharePoint environment and have identified threats to the key components of your environment, the next step is to develop your SharePoint DR plan.

 One thing that you should never do is create your SharePoint DR plan in a vacuum. This means you should not develop your SharePoint DR plan without input and feedback from other key stakeholders, whether they are IT stakeholders or business stakeholders.

Your SharePoint DR plan should be part of a larger **business continuity plan (BCP)**, which is typically driven by business stakeholders. The BCP will identify what websites and components within the SharePoint environment are most critical, and what the acceptable levels of downtime are for these items. The BCP should also contain the plan for communicating any downtime to the end users.

Identifying key stakeholders

The first step in creating an effective SharePoint DR plan is to define the overall scope of the plan and to define the key components that must be restored in the event of a disaster. Having a well-defined scope, and knowing the key components, will allow for a more productive process of developing your SharePoint DR plan. You should begin by working with the key stakeholders within your organization that would be affected if your SharePoint environment were to become unavailable as a result of a disaster. In addition to the individuals responsible for administering and maintaining SharePoint itself, other key stakeholders will play a key role in developing the SharePoint DR plan.

IT

From an IT perspective, the key stakeholders are typically represented by individuals from the three key components of the physical architecture, namely servers, database, and network. In addition, there may be stakeholders from messaging and development, depending upon the configuration of your SharePoint environment, and if there is any custom developed code running in it.

Servers

The server support team will typically consist of individuals that are responsible for installing and maintaining the servers in your SharePoint environment, from an operating system and hardware perspective. This holds true for both physical and virtual servers, however, there may be other individuals responsible for installing and maintaining the virtual hosts if you have virtual servers in your SharePoint environment.

Database

The database support team will typically consist of DBAs who are responsible for installing, configuring, and maintaining the SQL Server databases in your SharePoint environment. The DBAs are often responsible for monitoring the health of the SQL servers, as well as creating and maintaining database level backup schedules.

Network

The network support team consists of individuals responsible for the connectivity between the systems and services that make up your SharePoint environment. Included in this group are the individuals responsible for configuring and maintaining DNS, hardware load balancers, and associated **virtual IP (VIP)** addresses.

Messaging

SharePoint supports both incoming and outgoing e-mails; therefore, if your SharePoint environment is using either or both, then there should be a stakeholder from the messaging support team to make sure that all matters regarding SharePoint and messaging are covered.

Development

The features and functionality of SharePoint can be enhanced and extended through custom developed features, solutions, and apps. If your SharePoint environment makes use of custom developed code then your stakeholders should include representatives from the development support team.

Business

From a business perspective, the number of key stakeholders can range from just one or two individuals in a small company to a significant number of individuals in a very large company. Regardless of the number of key business stakeholders, they will play the biggest role in defining the scope of your SharePoint DR plan. The key business stakeholders will identify the individual SharePoint websites and services that will need to be available, and how soon they will need to be available in the event of a disaster. The results of this **business impact analysis (BIA)** will be the foundation upon which your SharePoint DR plan will be developed.

The earlier examples of key stakeholders are typical of very large organizations. If you are working in a small or medium size organization these key stakeholders will most often be roles filled by the same person, or may not even be filled by anyone. For example, in a small organization there may not be a DBA. SQL Server may have been set up by an outside consulting organization that is no longer engaged with your organization.

Regardless of whether your organization has these key stakeholders or not, this section provides an example of the types of individuals and roles that will play a part in developing your SharePoint DR plan.

Developing the plan

Chapter 1, Planning and Key Concepts – What Not to Forget, describes two types of recovery objectives: RTO and RPO. The BIA will have a direct impact on the RTO and RPO goals of your SharePoint DR plan, as it will define the recovery targets of the individual components of your SharePoint environment.

Defining recovery targets

Recovery targets are defined as the key pieces of functionality and data identified in the BIA that needs to be restored in the event of a disaster, in relation to the components of your SharePoint environment identified earlier in this chapter. You will need to work with the key stakeholders to establish the recovery targets for each component of your SharePoint environment, in order to build your SharePoint DR plan.

In some cases, such as when you have a large SharePoint farm, your recovery targets may only represent a subset of the total functionality of the farm. This will certainly be the case if the RTO is very aggressive, and a full recovery will take more time than what the RTO will allow.

Understanding costs

It is important to remember that each decision made during the development of your SharePoint DR plan will have an associated cost. One must understand the cost of downtime, in order to understand the cost impact of how you handle a SharePoint disaster. If your SharePoint farm contains mission or business critical data or applications then the cost of downtime should be considered high. This means that the cost of developing a SharePoint DR plan that includes investments in additional hardware can be offset by the reduced duration of the downtime.

If you have a high RPO then you might need additional space for more frequent backups. This might mean an additional investment in storage space, third party backup/restore software, or an SQL Server with failover clustering, database mirroring, or AlwaysOn Availability Groups.

 AlwaysOn Availability Groups is a feature of SQL Server 2012. This is a high-availability and DR solution that provides an enterprise-level alternative to database mirroring that maximizes the availability of a set of user databases for an enterprise.

The following diagram shows a SharePoint farm configured for high availability. It shows how complex a SharePoint farm can get if you are building for high availability. Looking at the number of servers and components involved in a high availability farm shows just how costly this kind of solution could be.

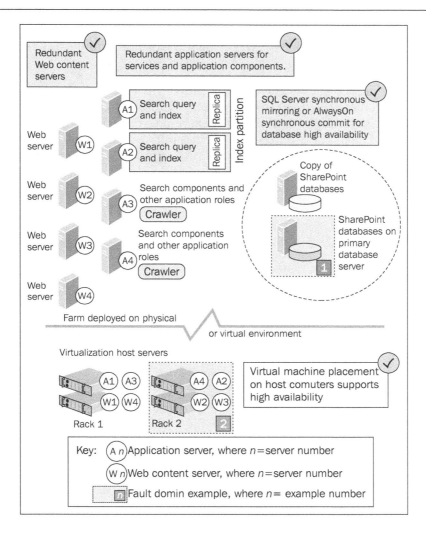

Planning for **high availability (HA)** requires redundancy in your physical architecture, such as failover SQL clusters and redundant application servers. It is important to know that HA could have some significant costs associated with it, depending upon which components of your physical architecture you will build for HA.

If you have a high RTO and RPO, you might need to invest in a secondary datacenter or failover farm with cold standby, warm standby, or hot standby, as described in *Chapter 1*, *Planning and Key Concepts – What Not to Forget*.

The following diagram shows a SharePoint farm with a redundant farm in a secondary datacenter. The diagram shows the redundant farm and how it is physically and potentially geographically separated from your primary farm. The advantage of this kind of redundancy comes into play in the event of a disaster in which you lose your primary datacenter. An example of this would be in the event of a natural disaster, such as a hurricane or flood, where you could lose your primary datacenter. Your physically and geographically separated datacenter is unaffected, so it would then become your primary datacenter until your primary datacenter is back up and running.

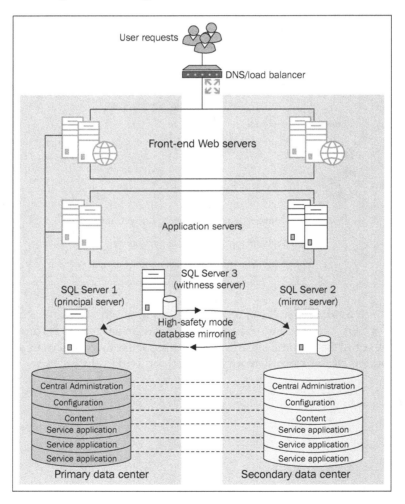

Virtualization

Virtualization provides a workable, cost-effective option for a recovery solution. You can use virtualization technology such as Hyper-V or VMware as an on-premise solution or you can use tools such as Windows Azure or **Amazon Web Services** (**AWS**) as a hosted solution, to provide necessary infrastructure for recovery.

You can create virtual images of the production servers and ship these images to a secondary datacenter. By using the virtual standby solution, you have to make sure that the virtual images are created often enough to provide the level of farm configuration and content freshness that you must have for recovering the farm in order to meet your recovery targets and RTO and RPO goals.

A virtual standby solution maintains up-to-date standby virtual machines for fast push-button DR. The bootable virtual machine is an exact clone of the production server as of the last snapshot or backup.

For more information on backups or snapshots in a virtual environment, refer to *Chapter 4, Virtual Environment Backup and Restore Procedures.*

Service level agreements

A **Service level agreement** (**SLA**) is a written agreement that specifies the requirements for server or application uptime and the penalties for not meeting those requirements. Two of the most specific and important components within an SLA are RPO and RTO. Both components are extremely important in developing your SharePoint DR plan.

The RPO is retroactive from the moment of actual failure. It can be set in seconds, minutes, hours, or days, but must correspond to the amount of tolerable lost data.

The RTO is typically based on lost revenue or productivity measured in seconds, minutes, hours, or days and corresponds to the measurable uptime (99.99%, 99.999% and so on) within an SLA.

The following table shows a very basic sample SharePoint SLA:

SERVICE ITEM	SERVICE COMMITMENT
Availability	99.9%
RTO	< 5 hours
RPO	30 minute data loss window

[Although a SharePoint SLA contains many more service items, the above sample shows the available components only.]

Planning for recovery

Now that you have set the RPO and RTO for your SharePoint environment, established the recovery targets, and understand the costs associated with these recovery targets, it's time to begin planning for recovery. Recovery is defined as the steps that must be taken in order to get the SharePoint environment back to an acceptable level of functionality as defined in the BIA.

[Make sure that your plan for recovery includes a communications plan. It will be important to keep the key stakeholders as well as end users up to date on the recovery process, especially if there are mission critical applications that have been affected by the disaster.]

Recovery resources

In order to begin planning for recovery you must begin by identifying the resources, such as people, hardware, and software, that will be needed to start the recovery process.

People

Your SharePoint DR plan should include a list of key individuals and stakeholders that will be part of the recovery process. This list should include the following:

- Name
- Department
- Role
- Primary phone number
- Backup phone number
- e-mail address
- Recovery responsibilities

Hardware

Once you have established what additional hardware will be needed for recovery, you should begin the process of acquiring the hardware so that it is in hand as soon as possible. Whether the hardware is dedicated hardware or shared hardware, make sure it is clearly identified as hardware associated with the SharePoint recover process.

Software

If any additional software is required for a secondary datacenter or failover farm then you must acquire and maintain a sufficient amount of licenses to support the secondary datacenter or failover farm, in accordance with the software vendor's licensing policy.

You also need to ensure that you maintain a copy of each service pack, patch, hotfix, and **Cumulative Update** (**CU**) installed on your farm. Sometimes hotfixes are superseded later by other hotfixes, or even retracted and can no longer be downloaded in the original form, so maintaining copies will ensure that you can return to the exact patch level you had before you had the disaster, if you find yourself in a DR scenario.

Dependent services

SharePoint depends on a number of services that may not be covered by the SharePoint DR plan. Services such as SQL Server, AD, DNS, and SMTP might have their own individual DR plans. It is important to make sure that the RTO and RPO values for these services are in line with those of the SharePoint environment. If they are not in line with each other then you must look at what needs to be done to get them in line, even if this means adjusting the RTO and RPO of the SharePoint environment, or increasing the budget set aside for the SharePoint DR plan.

Establishing and documenting your recovery procedures

The next step in developing your SharePoint DR plan is to establish and document the procedures required for recovery. It is important to document these procedures as clearly and concisely as possible, with the understanding that the individual or individuals executing these procedures may not have been a part of developing the SharePoint DR plan. They are also most likely to be under a great deal of pressure during the execution of the plan, so the more clearly the procedures are written, the better the chance of success within the expected timelines.

It is important to communicate your SharePoint DR plan so those that have a stake in the plan or will be a part of the testing or execution of the plan are aware of it and know where to go to see the latest copy as you SharePoint DR plan will be an ever-evolving and changing document.

Defining success criteria

How do you know that your recovery is a success without defining success criteria? The criteria for determining whether your recovery was a success or not should be clearly defined in your SharePoint DR plan. Typically, success criteria are derived from the recovery targets established during the development of the plan. For example, if you have a recovery target for the corporate intranet defined as one business day, then if during executing or testing your SharePoint DR plan you are able to have your corporate intranet up and running in one business day or less, the recovery is considered a success.

Success criteria can vary for different applications and websites that are part your SharePoint farm. As you are defining your recovery targets when developing your DR plan, you will identify the various components of your SharePoint farm, including individual application and websites, and what will define a successful recovery for each of these components in the event of a disaster.

Reviewing the plan

Once you have completed your SharePoint DR plan, it is important that the plan is thoroughly reviewed for accuracy and clarity. This review should be completed by a third party, or if that's not possible, a qualified person, or group that was not involved with creating the plan.

You should never consider your SharePoint DR plan complete until it has been checked and verified by parties that were not involved with creating the plan.

For more information, please navigate to the page titled "Plan for high availability and DR for SharePoint 2013" at `http://technet.microsoft.com/en-us/library/cc263031.aspx`.

Testing your DR plan

After taking the time to create a SharePoint DR plan, the last thing you should do is file it away (outside of your SharePoint environment) and hope you never have to use it. You need to confirm that the plan works as expected, so if or when the time comes to activate the plan, you and the stakeholders have confidence that the plan, if executed properly, will deliver the expected results.

 As a best practice you should test your DR plan on an ongoing basis. It is recommended that larger organizations test their DR plan at least twice a year. Smaller organizations should test their DR plan annually.

Planning your test

Testing your SharePoint DR plan will help you to identify any missing steps, potential problems with existing steps, missing dependencies, and potential bottlenecks. Testing will also help you to determine the timings associated with each step of the recovery plan, so that you know whether the plan will meet your RTO and RPO goals.

It is important to determine when and where your tests will be conducted. You should try to conduct your tests in an environment that resembles your normal production environment, so that you can get a realistic feel for the plan and how it will work if your production environment went down.

Determining your test scopes

In order to test your SharePoint DR plan, you need to define the scope of the tests you will be conducting. Begin by identifying the types of outages that your SharePoint environment may experience. Some examples of common types of outages are as follows:

- Configuration database corruption
- Content database corruption
- Server failure:
    - Application server
    - Database server
    - Web front end
- Virtual host failure
- Datacenter failure

For each test, the appropriate resources will be needed to help conduct the test and determine if the test was a success. For example, you may be testing the scenario of a failed application server, and your plan calls for the relevant services that were running on the failed server to be moved to a server that is still up and running in the farm. In this scenario, once the services have been moved and configured, the appropriate resources would need to validate that the services are up and running, and that the SharePoint farm is behaving as expected.

Performing the test

Once you have finished planning your test, and your test scopes have been defined, you need to perform a full test of your SharePoint DR plan.

Your tests should be conducted in the context of the overall BCP, so that you get a feel for how the plan fits in and works with your company's BCP. Involve your key stakeholders from both IT and business, and be sure to include the communications plan.

All tests should be thoroughly documented by creating a checklist to record the following information for each test and each step within a test:

- Test ID (sequentially numbered, for example, 001, 002, 003, and so on)
- Test name
- Test description
- DR plan reference:
    - Step ID
    - Step description
    - Expected results
    - Actual results
    - Expected duration
    - Actual duration
    - Pass/Fail
    - Comments

Analysing the results

Once you have completed all of the tests in your test scope, it is time to go back and analyze the test results. In all cases, you will be measuring the results of the test against the defined success criteria, including the RTO and RPO goals.

Regardless of whether the test passed or failed, all test results should be well documented, and shared with the key stakeholders, so that everyone has an understanding of what worked and what did not.

Maintaining your DR plan

Your SharePoint DR plan should be considered a living document, which means that it will continue to evolve over time as your farm continues to grow and new technologies are introduced into the environment.

Over time, you may find that budget constraints that at one point limited your RTO and RPO goals may no longer be a concern and your RTO and RPO goals can be adjusted accordingly, as new funding is made available for things such as a standby datacenter.

You should schedule periodic reviews of the plan and adjust the plan as necessary. It is important to continue to test your SharePoint DR plan as it evolves over time.

For example, you should plan to review your SharePoint DR plan at least once a quarter. You should review all aspects of the SharePoint DR plan, including your recovery targets, RTO, and RPO.

You should plan on performing a full test of your SharePoint DR plan at least once or twice a year, depending upon the size of your organization, number of systems to be tested, amount of data to be recovered, and the complexity of your SharePoint DR plan.

After each test, you will need to update your SharePoint DR plan according to the results of your test. This will ensure that your SharePoint DR plan is properly maintained and will be ready in the event of a disaster.

Downloading the inventory worksheet

You can download the inventory worksheet for this book from http://www.packtpub.com. If you purchased this book elsewhere, you can visit http://www.packtpub.com/support and register to have the files e-mailed directly to you.

Further reading

An overview of SharePoint 2013 installation and configuration is available at:

`http://technet.microsoft.com/en-us/library/ee667264.aspx`

Technical diagrams for SharePoint 2013 are available at:

`http://technet.microsoft.com/en-us/library/cc263199.aspx`

The technical reference for SharePoint 2013 is available at:

`http://technet.microsoft.com/en-us/library/cc262798.aspx`

Summary

This chapter has defined what it takes to create, test, and maintain a SharePoint DR plan. As you can see, this is not a 30 minute exercise where one person creates, tests, and maintains the DR plan alone, but an ongoing activity that has a number of stakeholders and key individuals who will be responsible for ensuring that your organization is continually working to have the best plan in place, in case of a SharePoint disaster.

The next chapter explains physical backup and restore procedures for the SharePoint environment.

3
Physical Backup and Restore Procedures

The previous chapter discussed about creating, testing, and maintaining the DR plan. It explained that it is not a 30-minute exercise where one person creates, tests, and maintains the DR plan alone, but an ongoing activity that has a number of stakeholders and key individuals who will be responsible for ensuring that your organization is continually working to have the best plan in place, in case of a SharePoint disaster.

This chapter introduces the reader to the backup and recovery activities of SharePoint DR that relate to the following:

- Windows Server 2012 – system state data backup, partitioning of data, and loss of data
- SQL backup and restore – system database backup and restore, third-party database backup and restore, point-in-time backup and restore
- SQL Server databases – SQL Server Management Studio, PowerShell, and non-SharePoint backup and restore
- Advanced backup techniques – backing up large farms, PowerShell to speed up performance and restoring

Windows Server 2012

This section focuses on the mechanics of performing a backup of the server, using **Out of Box** (**OOB**) server tools for backups.

System state data backup

The **System State Data** (**SSD**) is an operating system layer that backs up the SharePoint server, which is crucial. It is not enough to just backup your data; the SSD backups maintain a copy of configuration and identity of the server. This includes the following files:

- The registry
- COM+ registration
- Boot and system files
- IIS meta-directory

In short, this is the most important type of backup because the SharePoint environment works from the SSD configurations. This data also needs to be in sync across all the server environments.

 Installation of new programs or hardware is recorded in the registry.

Service packs and hotfixes overwrite the system files; so changes to web configuration may cause an update in the meta-directory.

 Backups of SSD should be performed when significant changes are made in one of the areas stated previously.

While SSD backups should be scheduled on a regular basis, performing a backup before and after any changes are made is extremely important.

Server backups are not used to restore SharePoint, but rather to restore the server with as little downtime as possible. After restoration of your Windows Server, you would restore SQL Server and then SharePoint.

Partitioning of data

A server backup plan will be only as good as the storage plan supporting it.

 This scenario abstracts the physical disk configuration. Volume may refer to different physical disks or logical divisions on hardware such as RAID, SAN, NAS, or any other performance disaster recovery configuration.

The following table shows a typical storage-partitioning scheme for a server hosting SharePoint that has four volumes:

Volume	Contents
C:	Windows operating system
D:	Installed applications, including SQL Server, SharePoint, and other supporting software
E:	SQL Server data files (.MDF, .NDF)
F:	SQL Server transaction log files (.LDF)

The first volume (C:) listed in the previous table hosts the Windows operating system. The second volume (D:) is the target volume for the installation of programs. It includes the binaries for SQL and other locally installed applications. The third volume (E:) hosts the data files (MDFs and NDFs). The fourth volume holds transaction logs. This scenario does not specify placement of the IIS website directory. Depending on the solution, there are a few options.

From the server backup perspective, only the first two volumes are of primary concern. Backup of data on C: along with an SSD backup are all that is needed to restore the server to the same or a similar hardware. Backups of C: will be done in regularly scheduled maintenance packages. In addition, changes to critical services or applications will warrant C: and SSD backups.

The D: is also an important target for server backups. Registry pointers to binaries have little value if the targets don't exist. While C: should be backed up regularly, D: does not require frequent backups. There is no configuration or data on the application partition. This backup only needs to be updated when a program is installed, patched, or removed.

 The crown jewels of the SharePoint server are on E:. This volume must be protected with more vigilance than the others.

On this drive are the enterprise's collaboration, storage, and online workspace. Though crucial, there are better tools to back up the SharePoint data than server backups. Protecting the data files and log files is an upcoming topic.

Full backups of the C: and D: volumes will allow restoration of the server, with all software and identity information in the same state as just prior to failure. Restoration of C: resets the registry and ensures that the machine has the same local and Active Directory identity. Restoration of D: brings in the binaries and supporting files for all of the software loaded on the system.

By separating the data from the supporting software, you allow an administrator to restore the server to a functional state rapidly. Less data will be redundantly restored, meaning that little time is lost restoring the same components multiple times.

 Any corruption of the operating system or misconfiguration of a service would result in a restoration of only the C:. If a loss of drives was the cause of the restoration, then restoring the C: and D: volumes would result in a fully-operational server, with software and hardware configured.

Additional precautions can be taken to support alternative recovery scenarios. Even though the previous scenario is a solid disaster recovery plan in most situations, the value of the data may necessitate supplemental precautions. There are a handful of niche disaster recovery tools included with the Windows Server that may be appropriate.

System database backup and restore

Backing up SQL Server system databases (everything) will restore and recover the SQL Server system in the event of a system failure, such as the loss of a hard disk. The system databases backup include msdb, master, and model. If replication is being used, the distribution database is required.

 The backup frequency and retention are usually based on the company's policy. As a general rule of thumb, take a daily full backup, followed by before and after backups when adding a new database or making structural changes to the SQL Server instance.

Backing up DB using SQL Server Management Studio

1. Connect to your instance in the SQL Server database engine; on the left hand side, click on the server name to expand the tree.

2. Click on the + to collapse the databases, then depending on the database, either select a user database or expand **System Databases** and select a system database.

3. Right-click on the database, point to **Tasks**, and then click on **Back Up**. The **Backup Database** dialog box will appear.

4. In the **Database** listbox, verify the database name.

5. You can perform a backup of the following recovery models:
    ° FULL
    ° BULK_LOGGED
    ° SIMPLE

6. In the Backup type listbox, select the module you want to use.

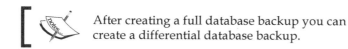 After creating a full database backup you can create a differential database backup.

7. You can also select **Copy Only Backup**. A copy only backup is an SQL server backup that is independent of the sequence of conventional SQL server backups.

 When the **Differential** option is selected, you cannot create a copy-only backup.

8. For the backup component, click on **Database**.

9. Either accept the default backup set name in the textbox, or enter a different name for the backup set.

10. Enter a description of the backup set.

11. Specify when the backup set will expire and can be overwritten:
    1. To have the backup set expire after a specific number of days, click on After (the default option), and enter the number of days after set creation that the set will expire, a value of 0 days means that the backup set will never expire.
    2. The default value is set to backup media retention in days. To access this, right-click on the server name in the left-hand side and select properties; then select the Database Settings page.

12. To choose the destination click on Disk or Tape and select the paths of up to 64 disk or tape drives contained in a single media set, and then click on **Add**. The selected paths are displayed in the **Backup to** listbox.

13. In the **Reliability** section, optionally check the following:
    ° Verify backup when finished
    ° Perform checksum before writing to media

14. If you are backing up to a tape drive, the **Unload the tape after backup** option is active. Clicking on this option activates **Rewind the tape** before unloading option.

15. SQL Server 2008 Enterprise and later supports backup compression.

> For information on copy-only backups (SQL Server), visit
> `http://msdn.microsoft.com/en-us/library/`
> `f82d6918-a5a7-4af8-868e-4247f5b00c52`
>
> For information on backup compression (SQL Server), visit
> `http://msdn.microsoft.com/en-us/library/`
> `bb964719.aspx`

Backing up DB using PowerShell

The advantages of using PowerShell to back up SQL databases are as follows:

- Backup/restore scripts can be developed and scheduled with the Windows Task Scheduler, whereas central administration is used for single-use backups and restores.

- There is the advantage of running against SQL snapshots instead of the production database. One of the parameters of the Windows PowerShell command will cause a SQL snapshot to be generated, and then Windows PowerShell will run the action against the snapshot instead of the production database. This will reduce the resource impact of the backup operation on the production environment.

- There is more granular control of options for the backup or restore.

The following script takes the server instance and the location of the backups as variable inputs. The script will back up all the system databases except the `tempdb` databases. The `tempdb` is recreated every time SQL Server instance is started, and therefore it does not need to be backed up.

```
# Variable inputs
$SQLInstance = "sqlserver01"
$BackupFolder = "\\servername\"
$tStamp = Get-Date -format yyyy_MM_dd_HHmmss


[System.Reflection.Assembly]::LoadWithPartialName(
  "Microsoft.SqlServer.SMO") | Out-Null
[System.Reflection.Assembly]::LoadWithPartialName(
  "Microsoft.SqlServer.SmoExtended") | Out-Null
$srv = New-Object (
```

```
        "Microsoft.SqlServer.Management.Smo.Server") $SQLInstance
$dbs = New-Object Microsoft.SqlServer.Management.Smo.Database
$dbs = $srv.Databases
foreach ($Database in $dbs | where {$_.IsSystemObject -eq $True })
{
  if ($Database.name -ne "tempdb")
  {
    $Database.name
    $bk = New-Object ("Microsoft.SqlServer.Management.Smo.Backup")
    $bk.Action =
      [Microsoft.SqlServer.Management.Smo.BackupActionType]::Database
    $bk.BackupSetName = $Database.Name + "_backup_" + $tStamp
    $bk.Database = $Database.Name
    $bk.CompressionOption = 1
    $bk.MediaDescription = "Disk"
    $bk.Devices.AddDevice($BackupFolder + "\" + $Database.Name +
      "_" + $tStamp + ".bak", "File")
    TRY
    {
      $bk.SqlBackup($srv)
    }
    CATCH
    {
      $Database.Name + " backup failed."
      $_.Exception.Message}
  }
}
```

Restoring master DB with SQL Server Management Studio

In order to restore the master databases, you need to have an instance of SQL Server running, an operational master database for the instance to start. If the current master database is corrupted, a new one must be created using the original media of SQL Server 2012.

To restore a database backup with SQL Server Management Studio follow these steps:

1. Connect to your instance in the SQL Server Database Engine; on the left-hand side, click on the server name to expand the tree.

2. Click on the **+** to collapse the databases, then depending on the database, either select a user database or expand **System Databases** and select a system database.

3. Right-click on the database, point to **Tasks,** and click on **Restore.**

4. Click on the database that opens in the **Restore Database** dialog box.

5. On the **General** page, the name of the restoring database appears in the **To database** listbox.

6. In the **To a point in time** textbox, you can leave as **Most recent possible** or select a specific date and time by clicking the browse button; this opens the **Point in Time Restore** dialog box.

7. To specify the source and location of the backup sets to restore, click on one of the following options:

   ° From database

   ° Enter a database name

   ° From device

8. Select the backup sets to restore grid and then select the backup to restore. Here you will see all of the backups that are available. By default, a recovery plan is suggested. To override the suggested recovery plan, just change the selections in the grid. Any backups that depend on a deselected backup are deselected automatically.

9. You can also choose to restore the database to a new location by specifying the new restore destination.

10. The recovery state panel determines the state of the database after the restore is complete.

Restoring master DB with PowerShell

To start the server instance in single-user mode, run the following command in PowerShell or command prompt:

```
NET STOP MSSQLSERVER
NET START MSSQLSERVER /f /T3608
```

To restore a full database backup of the master database, use the following commands:

```
Import-Module SQLPS
$serverinstance="hostname/intacename"
$databasename="master"
$backupfilepath="\\share\folder\master.bak"
Restore-SqlDatabase -ServerInstance $serverinstance -Database
$databasename -BackupFile $backupfilepath -ReplaceDatabase
```

Also see PowerShell changes for database backups in SQL
Server 2012 at

`http://www.mssqltips.com/sqlservertip/2572/`
`powershell-changes-for-database-backups-in-`
`sql-server-2012/`

Non-SharePoint database backup and restore

For many developers, it is very appealing to add their solutions to custom
databases hosted on the farm database server, as it seems a logical solution
because the application or integration process is part of SharePoint. SQL
Server backups are the most reliable product.

The authors recommend using a SQL Server maintenance plan schedule
for full backups, or if the organization uses an enterprise schedule system,
use PowerShell. See the following samples:

Backing up DB with SQL Server Management Studio

To perform a backup with SQL Server Management Studio, perform the
following steps:

1. Open SQL Server Management Studio and connect to the SQL Server
   database instance hosting the SharePoint database that is required to be
   backed up.

2. Expand the **Databases**. Right-click on the name of the database, select the
   Tasks option when the menu opens, click on the **Back Up** option to open
   the **Back Up Database** dialog box.

3. On the **General** page, select the source database for the backup and
   determine the backup type, the components to be backed up, the backup
   set associated with the backup, and the destination for the file(s) created
   by the backup operation.

4. The **Options** page allows the configuration settings for overwriting existing backup files, backup reliability, handling of transaction logs and tape drives by the backup operation, and compression option.

5. After the backup settings have been configured, click on the **OK** button to start the backup operation.

Backing up DB with PowerShell

In PowerShell it is possible to replicate steps found in the Management Studio. In the following sample, the script backs up a list of databases to disk and uses backup compression. The backup files are created using the database name and time stamp.

```
$SQLInstance = "nj-srv-sqlmgt"
$BackupFolder = "D:\tmp"
$dbs =@("Database names"," Database names");

$tStamp = Get-Date -format yyyy_MM_dd_HHmmss
[System.Reflection.Assembly]::LoadWithPartialName("
  Microsoft.SqlServer.SMO") | Out-Null
[System.Reflection.Assembly]::LoadWithPartialName("
  Microsoft.SqlServer.SmoExtended") | Out-Null
$srv = New-Object ("Microsoft.SqlServer.Management.Smo.Server")
  $SQLInstance


foreach ($Database in $dbs )
{

  $Database
  $bk = New-Object ("Microsoft.SqlServer.Management.Smo.Backup")
  $bk.Action = [Microsoft.SqlServer.Management.
    Smo.BackupActionType]::Database
  $bk.BackupSetName = $Database + "_backup_" + $tStamp
  $bk.Database = $Database
  $bk.CompressionOption = 1
  $bk.MediaDescription = "Disk"
  $bk.Devices.AddDevice($BackupFolder + "\" + $Database + "_" +
    $tStamp + ".bak", "File")
  TRY
  {
    $bk.SqlBackup($srv)
  }
  CATCH
  {
```

```
     $Database + " backup failed."
     $_.Exception.Message
  }


}
```

To back up all databases including system databases, run the following script:

```
$SQLInstance = "sqlserver01"
$BackupFolder = "\\servername\"
$tStamp = Get-Date -format yyyy_MM_dd_HHmmss
[System.Reflection.Assembly]::LoadWithPartialName(
  "Microsoft.SqlServer.SMO") | Out-Null
[System.Reflection.Assembly]::LoadWithPartialName(
  "Microsoft.SqlServer.SmoExtended") | Out-Null
$srv = New-Object (
  "Microsoft.SqlServer.Management.Smo.Server") $SQLInstance
$dbs = New-Object Microsoft.SqlServer.Management.Smo.Database
$dbs = $srv.Databases
foreach ($Database in $dbs)
{
  if ($Database.name -ne "tempdb")
  {
    $Database.name
    $bk = New-Object
      ("Microsoft.SqlServer.Management.Smo.Backup")
    $bk.Action = [Microsoft.SqlServer.
      Management.Smo.BackupActionType]::Database
    $bk.BackupSetName = $Database.Name + "_backup_" + $tStamp
    $bk.Database = $Database.Name
    $bk.CompressionOption = 1
    $bk.MediaDescription = "Disk"
    $bk.Devices.AddDevice($BackupFolder + "\" + $Database.Name +
      "_" + $tStamp + ".bak", "File")
    TRY
    {
      $bk.SqlBackup($srv)
    }
    CATCH
    {
      $Database.Name + " backup failed."
      $_.Exception.Message
    }
  }
}
```

Restore

The following outlines the steps to perform a SQL restore with Management Studio and PowerShell.

Restoring master DB with SQL Server Management Studio

In order to restore the master databases, you need to have an instance of a SQL Server running, and the master database needs to be operational in order for the instance to start. If the current master database is corrupted, a new one must be created by using the original media of SQL Server 2012.

To restore a database backup with SQL Server Management Studio, carry out the following steps:

1. Connect to your instance in the SQL Server Database Engine; on the left-hand side, click on the server name to expand the tree.

2. Click on the **+** to collapse the databases, then depending on the database, either select a user database or expand **System Databases** and select a system database.

3. Right-click on the database, point to **Tasks**, and click on Restore.

4. Click on the database that opens in the **Restore Database** dialog box.

5. On the **General** page, the name of the restoring database appears in the **To database** listbox.

6. In the **To a point in time** textbox, you can leave **Most recent possible** or select a specific date and time by clicking on the browse button, this opens the **Point in Time Restore** dialog box.

7. To specify the source and location of the backup sets to restore, click one of the following options:
   - From database
   - Enter a database name
   - From device

8. Select the backup sets to restore grid, and then select the backup to restore. Here you will see all the backups that are available. By default, a recovery plan is suggested. To override the suggested recovery plan, just change the selections in the grid. Any backups that depend on a deselected backup are deselected automatically.

9. You can also choose to restore the database to a new location by specifying a new restore destination.

10. The recovery state panel determines the state of the database after the restore is complete.

Restoring DB with PowerShell

The following script restores a single database from the last successful full backup:

```
Import-Module SQLPS
$serverinstance="hostname/intacename"
$databasename="dbname"
$backupfilepath=\\share\folder\MyDB.bak

Restore-SqlDatabase -ServerInstance $serverinstance -Database
$databasename -BackupFile $backupfilepath
```

Point in time backup and restore

Every once in a while, an event might happen that corrupts a database and a database backup is required. If there is at least a complete database backup then the corrupted database is recoverable. However, if this backup is corrupted then a point in time restore is required.

 A point in time recovery is a method to recover a database to any point in time since the last database backup.

SQL Server has the ability to recover the data point in time from the last committed transition before the system crashed.

Incremental backups require the database to run on full recovery mode. This means that every transaction will be stored on the transactional logs and it must be backed up in order to be overwritten. Depending on the load, some transactional logs can grow up to 100 GB if they are not backed up frequently.

Point in time backup and restore can be performed with Management Studio and PowerShell.

Backing up DB in SQL Server Management Studio with SQL statements

To back up a database in SQL Server Management Studio with SQL statements, follow these steps:

1. Open SQL Management Studio.

2. Go to **New query** and connect the SharePoint SQL Server instance, and then type the following SQL statements:

```
BACKUP DATABASE DatabaseName
TO DISK = '\\servername\SQLServerBackups\DatabaseName.Bak'
With COMPRESSION, INIT

BACKUP DATABASE DatabaseName
TO DISK = '\\servername\SQLServerBackups\DatabaseName.Bak'
With DIFFERENTIAL, COMPRESSION, INIT

BACKUP LOG DatabaseName

TO DISK = '\\servername\SQLServerBackups\DatabaseName.trn'

With COMPRESSION
```

3. The following sample will generate an incremental backup SQL script which will include all databases with full recovery mode:

```
Declare @tstamp varchar(20)
declare @filelocation varchar(20)

set @tstamp= ( select '/'+ replace(replace(convert(nvarchar(50),
getdate(), 120), ':','.'),' ','T'))
set @filelocation ='\\servername\SQLServerBackups\'
select

'BACKUP LOG ' + Name +  ' TO DISK = '+@filelocation+Name+@
tstamp+'.trn'' With COMPRESSION ' + CHAR(13) + CHAR(10 )+ 'GO ' +
CHAR(13)

from sys.databases

where recovery_model_desc= 'full'
```

 Refer to How to: Restore to a Point in Time (SQL Server Management Studio) at http://msdn.microsoft.com/en-us/library/ms190982(v=SQL.105).aspx

Backing up SQL DB with PowerShell

To perform a full database backup using PowerShell, use the following script:

```
$SQLInstance = "sqlserver01"
$BackupFolder = "\\servername\"
$tStamp = Get-Date -format yyyy_MM_dd_HHmmss
[System.Reflection.Assembly]::LoadWithPartialName("Microsoft.
SqlServer.SMO") | Out-Null
[System.Reflection.Assembly]::LoadWithPartialName("Microsoft.
SqlServer.SmoExtended") | Out-Null
$srv = New-Object ("Microsoft.SqlServer.Management.Smo.Server")
$SQLInstance
$dbs = New-Object Microsoft.SqlServer.Management.Smo.Database
$dbs = $srv.Databases
foreach ($Database in $dbs | where {$_.RecoveryModel -ne "Simple"})
{
  $Database.name
  $bk = New-Object ("Microsoft.SqlServer.Management.Smo.Backup")
  $bk.Action = [Microsoft.SqlServer.
    Management.Smo.BackupActionType]::Database
  $bk.BackupSetName = $Database.Name + "_backup_" + $tStamp
  $bk.Database = $Database.Name
  $bk.CompressionOption = 1
  $bk.MediaDescription = "Disk"
  $bk.Devices.AddDevice($BackupFolder + "\" + $Database.Name +
    "_" + $tStamp + ".bak", "File")
  TRY
  {
    $bk.SqlBackup($srv)
  }
  CATCH
  {
    $Database.Name + " backup failed."
    $_.Exception.Message
  }
}
```

To perform a differential backup using PowerShell, use the following script:

```
$SQLInstance = "nj-srv-sqlmgt"
$BackupFolder = "D:\tmp"
$tStamp = Get-Date -format yyyy_MM_dd_HHmmss
[System.Reflection.Assembly]::LoadWithPartialName("Microsoft.
SqlServer.SMO") | Out-Null
[System.Reflection.Assembly]::LoadWithPartialName("Microsoft.
SqlServer.SmoExtended") | Out-Null
$srv = New-Object ("Microsoft.SqlServer.Management.Smo.Server")
$SQLInstance
$dbs = New-Object Microsoft.SqlServer.Management.Smo.Database
```

```
$dbs = $srv.Databases
foreach ($Database in $dbs | where {$_.RecoveryModel -ne "Simple"})
{
$Database.name
$bk = New-Object ("Microsoft.SqlServer.Management.Smo.Backup")
$bk.Action = [Microsoft.SqlServer.Management.Smo.
BackupActionType]::Database
$bk.BackupSetName = $Database.Name + "_backup_" + $tStamp
$bk.Database = $Database.Name
$bk.Incremental = $true
$bk.CompressionOption = 1
$bk.MediaDescription = "Disk"
$bk.Devices.AddDevice($BackupFolder + "\" + $Database.Name + "_" +
$tStamp + ".bak", "File")
TRY
{$bk.SqlBackup($srv)}
CATCH
{$Database.Name + " backup failed."
$_.Exception.Message}
}
```

To perform an incremental backup using PowerShell, use the following script:

```
$SQLInstance = "sqlserver01"
$BackupFolder = "\\servername\"
$tStamp = Get-Date -format yyyy_MM_dd_HHmmss
[System.Reflection.Assembly]::LoadWithPartialName("Microsoft.
SqlServer.SMO") | Out-Null
[System.Reflection.Assembly]::LoadWithPartialName("Microsoft.
SqlServer.SmoExtended") | Out-Null
$srv = New-Object ("Microsoft.SqlServer.Management.Smo.Server")
$SQLInstance
$dbs = New-Object Microsoft.SqlServer.Management.Smo.Database
$dbs = $srv.Databases
foreach ($Database in $dbs | where {$_.RecoveryModel -ne "Simple"})
{
$Database.name
$bk = New-Object ("Microsoft.SqlServer.Management.Smo.Backup")
$bk.Action = [Microsoft.SqlServer.Management.Smo.
BackupActionType]::Log
$bk.BackupSetName = $Database.Name + "_backup_" + $tStamp
$bk.Database = $Database.Name
$bk.CompressionOption = 1
$bk.MediaDescription = "Disk"
$bk.Devices.AddDevice($BackupFolder + "\" + $Database.Name + "_" +
$tStamp + ".trn", "File")
```

```
TRY
{$bk.SqlBackup($srv)}
CATCH
{$Database.Name + " backup failed."
$_.Exception.Message}
}
```

Restoring DB in SQL Server Management Studio with SQL statements

This section describes the process of restoring the database by using SQL statements. We will describe how to restore a database from a full differential and transaction log onto a database.

In this scenario, a database needs to be restored as of May 01, 2012 at 5:05 AM. Backup availability is as follows:

- Last full backup was done January 01, 2012 at 9:00 PM

- Last incremental backup was taken April 01, 2012 at 9:00 PM

- Incremental backups are taken every 5 hours after a full or differential backup, so apply the following incremental backups at 2 AM and 6 AM

Restore all the incremental backups since the last differential backup until the backup taken at a desired point in time.

To restore a full backup in SQL Server Management Studio with SQL Statement, follow these steps:

1. Open Management Studio

2. Go to **New query**, connect to the SharePoint SQL Server instance, and then type the following SQL statement to restore from the last full backup:

```
RESTORE DATABASE DatabaseName
FROM DISK = \\servername\SQLServerBackups\Fullbackup-DatabaseName.
Bak'
NORECOVERY;

Restore from last Differential backup

RESTORE DATABASE DatabaseName
  FROM DISK = \\servername\SQLServerBackups\differenctial
DatabaseName.Bak'
  NORECOVERY;
Restore from incremental backups up to 6 am

RESTORE LOG DatabaseName
```

```
FROM DISK ='\\servername\SQLServerBackups\2am_
incrementalDatabaseName.trn '

NORECOVERY, STOPAT = 'Jan 5, 2012 05:00 AM';

RESTORE LOG DatabaseName
FROM DISK ='\\servername\SQLServerBackups\6am_
incrementalDatabaseName.trn'
NORECOVERY, STOPAT = 'Jan 5, 2012 05:00 AM';


RESTORE DATABASE DatabaseName WITH RECOVERY;
```

Restoring SQL Server DB with PowerShell

For restoring SQL Server DB with PowerShell, use the following script:

```
Import-Module SQLPS
$serverinstance="hostname/intacename"
$databasename="dbname"
$Fullbackupfilepath="\\share\folder\Fullbackup-DatabaseName.Bak"

$differentialbackupfilepath="\\share\folder\differenctialDatabaseName.
Ba"
$incrementalbackupfilepath="\\share\folder\2am_
incrementalDatabaseName..trn"
$incrementalbackupfilepath2="\\share\folder\6am_
incrementalDatabaseName.trn"
$pointIntime= "Jan 5, 2012 05:00 AM"


Restore-SqlDatabase -ServerInstance $serverinstance -Database
$databasename -BackupFile $Fullbackupfilepath -NoRecovery

Restore-SqlDatabase -ServerInstance $serverinstance -Database
$databasename -BackupFile $differentialbackupfilepath -NoRecovery

Restore-SqlDatabase -ServerInstance $serverinstance -Database
$databasename -BackupFile $incrementalbackupfilepath -RestoreAction
Log -NoRecovery -ToPointInTime $pointIntime


Restore-SqlDatabase -ServerInstance $serverinstance -Database
$databasename -BackupFile $backupfilepath -RestoreAction Log
-ToPointInTime $pointIntime
```

Advanced backup techniques

Advanced backup techniques are often required when any environment has a large amount of content or the recovery service level agreements are of a short time frame.

Backing up large databases

In large environments with content databases that are over a TB, daily full farm backups could take more than 10 hours. Imagine receiving backup failures during full backups; it would take more than 20 hours to have a successful backup.

 There are many third-party tools, such as Symantec, EMC, and NetApp that have plugins to SharePoint and work very well.

The following section explains one common technique that uses farm backup and SQL Server backup combined.

Backup farm and SQL combined with PowerShell

Detach all the content databases for each web application and run a full farm backup. This should generally take less than 20 to 60 minutes depending on the size of the configuration databases and application databases. This technique works well when the full, differential, or incremental backup, is set to "On all databases". This technique also works well when RBS with the SQL FILESTREAM provider is being used.

See the following script:

```
$directory= "//servername/;

$nl = [Environment]::NewLine
$file = "webapp,URL,database";
$webapps= Get-SPWebApplication
foreach ( $webapp in $webapps )
{
  $webbappname=$webapp.Name
  $siteurl=$webapp.URL
  $ContentDatabases = $webapp.ContentDatabases
  foreach ( $ContentDatabase in $ContentDatabases)
  {
    $dbname=$ContentDatabase.Name;
```

```
        $line= "$nl$webbappname,$siteurl,$dbname"

        $file = $file + $line

    }

}
$file |Out-File $directory\sources.txt -Enc ascii

Get-SPWebApplication | %{$_.Name;$_.Url;%{
   $_.ContentDatabases|%{$_.Name};Write-Host ""}}

Get-SPContentDatabase | Dismount-SPContentDatabase -confirm:$false
Backup-SPFarm -Directory $directory -BackupMethod
   Full -BackupThreads 10 -Force

$data = Import-Csv $directory\sources.txt

foreach ( $db in $data)
{

  $app=$db.webapp
  $urlapp=$db.URL
  $dbname=$db.database

Mount-SPContentDatabase $dbname -DatabaseServer
   sqlservername -WebApplication $urlapp


}
```

Speeding up SQL Server backups

SQL Server can write to multiple files at the same time, and as a result, split up the workload. The advantage of this technique is that the backups run using multiple threads and finish faster, as well as moving across the network faster.

A PowerShell script that backs up and speeds up the SQL Server backup

The following script is used to speeds up the SQL Server backup:

```
$SQLInstance = "Instancename"
$BackupFolder = "\\servername\share"
$NumberofBackupsFiles=4

$tStamp = Get-Date -format yyyy_MM_dd_HHmmss
[System.Reflection.Assembly]::LoadWithPartialName(
    "Microsoft.SqlServer.SMO") | Out-Null
[System.Reflection.Assembly]::LoadWithPartialName(
    "Microsoft.SqlServer.SmoExtended") | Out-Null
$srv = New-Object (
    "Microsoft.SqlServer.Management.Smo.Server") $SQLInstance
#$dbs = New-Object Microsoft.SqlServer.Management.Smo.Database
$dbs = New-Object Microsoft.SqlServer.Management.Smo.Database
$dbs = $srv.Databases
foreach ($Database in $dbs)
{
  $Database.Name
  $bk = New-Object ("Microsoft.SqlServer.Management.Smo.Backup")
  $bk.Action = [Microsoft.SqlServer.Management
    .Smo.BackupActionType]::Database
  $bk.BackupSetName = $Database.Name + "_backup_" + $tStamp
  $bk.Database = $Database.Name
  $bk.CompressionOption = 1
  $bk.MediaDescription = "Disk"

  $i=1;
  do {
    $bk.Devices.AddDevice($BackupFolder + "\" +
      $Database.Name + $i + "_" + $tStamp + ".bak", "File");

    $i++
  }
  while ( $i -gt $NumberofBackupsFiles)

  TRY
  {
    $bk.SqlBackup($srv)
  }
  CATCH
  {
    $Database.Name + " backup failed."
    $_.Exception.Message
  }
}
```

Restoring databases with a different name

If the recovery of data is from an unattached content database from a different point in time, then restore the database with a different name.

PowerShell script to restore a database with a different name

The following sample restores an existing database backup to a new database name:

```
Import-Module SQLPS
$serverinstance="hostname/intacename"
$databasename="dbname_new"
$backupfilepath="\\share\folder\backupname.bak"
$newdatalocation ="d:\data\dbname_new.mdf"
$newloglocation ="e:\data\dbname_new.ldf"
$RelocateData = New-Object Microsoft.SqlServer.
  Management.Smo.RelocateFile("dbname_Data", $newloglocation)
$RelocateLog = New-Object Microsoft.SqlServer.
  Management.Smo.RelocateFile("dbname_Log", $RelocateLog)
Restore-SqlDatabase -ServerInstance $serverinstance -Database
$databasename -BackupFile $backupfilepath -RelocateFile @
($RelocateData,$RelocateLog)
```

Further reading

For more information, refer to the following articles:

- Charts of PowerShell commands to in total one or two pages of content: http://technet.microsoft.com/library/ff678226(office.15).aspx.

- How To: SQL Server Databases Backup with PowerShell: http://social.technet.microsoft.com/wiki/contents/articles/900.how-to-sql-server-databases-backup-with-powershell.aspx.

- From STSAdmin to PowerShell: http://technet.microsoft.com/en-us/library/ff621084(v=office.15).

- Database types and descriptions (SharePoint 2013): http://technet.microsoft.com/en-us/library/cc678868.aspx.

- Windows Server 2012 Hyper-V Cookbook: http://www.packtpub.com/windows-server-2012-hypervisor-based-cookbook/book.

- PowerShell 3.0 Advanced Administration: http://www.packtpub.com/powershell-3-0-advanced-administration-handbook/book.

Summary

This is one of the more lengthy chapters of the book, and has introduced the reader to the various approaches to backup and restore procedures for a physical SharePoint environment. But...wait, there is more to this topic. Backup and restore procedures for a virtual environment. This is explained in the following chapter.

4
Virtual Environment Backup and Restore Procedures

The last chapter discussed about Physical backup and restore procedures, this chapter is an extension of those procedures, and relates to virtual environments.

This chapter introduces you to backup and restore activities of SharePoint DR that relate to:

- Hyper-V and VMware
- Backup and restore
- Snapshots
- Failover clustering

Virtual environments

As explained in *Chapter 1, Planning and Key Concepts – What Not to Forget*, with virtualization technology, the server, including the operating system, applications, patches, and data are all encapsulated into a single image or virtual server. This image or virtual server can be backed up to an offsite DR datacentre and restored on another virtual host in a matter of minutes.

With more SharePoint implementations utilizing virtualization, it is important that a SharePoint DR strategy includes steps to take advantage of the backup and recovery capabilities of the virtualization technology your company has purchased. In this chapter, we will cover backup and recovery tools for the two most popular virtualization platforms, Microsoft Hyper-V and VMware vSphere 5.

Microsoft Hyper-V

Hyper-V is Microsoft's virtualization platform, available in Windows Server 2008, Windows Server 2008 R2, Windows Server 2012, and Windows Hyper-V Server 2012. It enables the creation of virtualized server computing environments for any or all of the components of a SharePoint environment. Hyper-V provides software infrastructure and basic management tools that can be used to create and manage a virtualized server-computing environment. The tools provided by Hyper-V include tools for backup and recovery.

Backup

In this section, we will show how to create a backup using Windows Server 2008/2008 R2 and Windows Server 2012.

Windows Server 2008 and Windows Server 2008 R2

It is possible to use the native Windows 2008 Backup to back up Hyper-V virtual servers, but Hyper-V provides VSS support that allows a zero downtime backup of virtual machines running Windows Server 2003 or Windows Server 2008/2008 R2, however, a backup program is required to take advantage of this.

To back up Hyper-V virtual servers from the parent partition on Windows Server 2008/2008 R2 by using **Windows Server Backup (WSB)**, register the Microsoft Hyper-V **Volume Shadow Copy Service (VSS)** writer with Windows Server Backup.

 To register the Microsoft Hyper-V VSS writer with Windows Server Backup automatically, go to http://go.microsoft.com/?linkid=9663637. Click on **Run** in the **File Download** dialog box, and then follow the steps in the wizard.

To back up a Hyper-V virtual machine follow these steps:

1. To access the backup and recovery tools, you must install the Windows Server Backup Features and subordinate items that are available in the **Add Features** wizard in **Server Manager**:

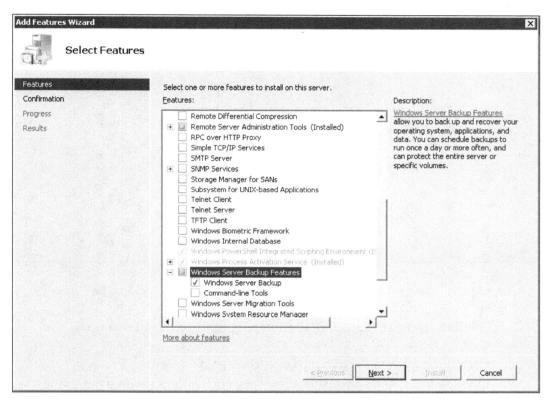

2. Once the **Windows Server Backup Features** are installed, open **Windows Server Backup** from the Administrative Tools folder.

3. In the **Actions** pane, click on **Backup Once**.

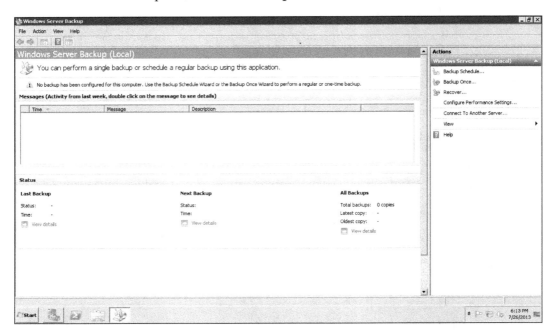

4. On the **Backup Options** page, navigate to **Different Options**, and then click on **Next**.

5. On the **Select Backup Configuration** page, navigate to **Custom**, and then click on **Next**.

6. In the **Select Items for Backup** page, click on **Add Items**.

7. In the **Select Items window**, click to select the volumes where the VM configuration files and VM hard disks are located.

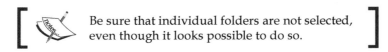

> Be sure that individual folders are not selected, even though it looks possible to do so.

8. Only select the entire volume. Once the volumes are selected, click on **OK**.

9. Back on the **Select Items for Backup** page, click on **Advanced Settings**.

10. In the **Advanced Settings** window, select **VSS Full Backup**, and then click on **OK**.

11. Back on the **Select Items for Backup** page, click on **OK**.

12. On the **Specify Destination Type** page, select the destination for the backup, and then click on **Next**.

13. On the **Select Backup Destination** page, use the drop-down list to select the destination, and then click on **OK**.

14. On the **Confirmation** page, click on **Backup** and the backup procedure will begin.

    Windows Server Backup begins to write the file(s) to the destination.

15. When the backup has finished, click on **Close**.

Windows Server 2012 and Windows Hyper-V Server 2012

Windows Server 2012 and Hyper-V Server 2012 come with a tool known as Windows Server Backup, which has full Hyper-V integration, allowing backup and restore of the server, applications, Hyper-V, and virtual machines.

To backup a Hyper-V virtual server follow these steps:

1. To access back up and recovery tools, you must install the **Windows Server Backup Features** and subordinate items that are available in the **Add Features** wizard in **Server Manager**:

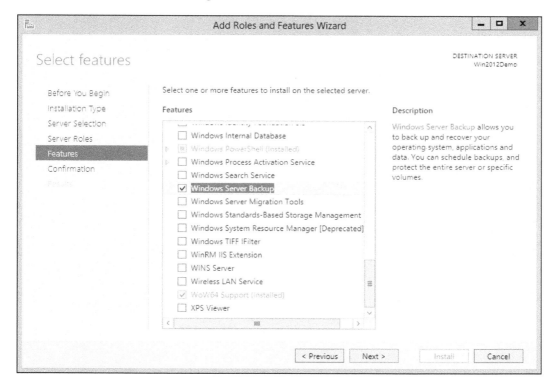

2. Once the **Windows Server Backup Features** are installed, open the **Start** menu and type wbadmin.msc to open the **Windows Server Backup** tool.

3. In the **Windows Server Backup** console, in the pane on the right-hand side, navigate to the **Backup**. The two available options are **Backup Schedule** to schedule an automatic backup and **Backup Once** for a single backup:

4. In the **Backup Schedule** wizard, on the **Getting Started** page, click on **Next**.

5. On the **Select Backup Configuration** page, navigate to **Full Server** to back up all the server data or click on **Custom** to select specific items to back up. If only Hyper-V and virtual machines are required for backup, click on **Custom**, and then click on **Next**.

6. On **Select Items for Backup**, click on **Add Items**.

7. In the **Select Items** window, select **Hyper-V** to back up all the virtual machines and the host components. Expand **Hyper-V** and select the virtual machines that are required to be backed up. When finished, click on **OK**.

8. Back on the **Select Items for Backup** page, click on **Advanced Settings** to change the **Exclusions** and **VSS Settings**.

9. In the **Advanced Settings** window, on the **Exclusions** tab, click on **Add Exclusion** to add any necessary exclusions.

10. Click on the **VSS Settings** tab to select either **VSS full Backup** or **VSS copy Backup**, and then click on **OK**.

11. In the **Select Items for Backup** window, confirm the items that will be backed up, and then click on **Next**.

12. On the **Specify Backup Time** page, select **Once a day** and the time for a daily backup, or select **More than once a day** and the time, and then click on **Next**.

13. On the **Specify Destination Type** page, select the option **Backup to a hard disk that is dedicated for backups (recommended)**, **Backup to a volume**, or **Backup to a shared network folder**, and then click on **Next**.

14. On **Select Destination Disk**, click on **Show All Available Disks** to list the disks, select the one that is required to store the backup, click on **OK**, and then click on **Next** twice.

15. If **Back up to a hard disk that is dedicated for backups (recommended)** option has been selected, there is a warning message saying that the disk will be formatted. Click on **Yes** to confirm.

16. In the **Confirmation** window, double-check the selected options, and then click on **Finish**.

17. The schedule will then be created. Wait until the scheduled start time, and check whether the backup has finished successfully.

Server recovery process

In this section, we will show how to recover a backup using Windows Server 2008/2008 R2 and Windows Server 2012.

Windows Server 2008 and Windows Server 2008 R2

Use the following steps to recover from backup containing virtual machines and the host components using Windows Server Backup:

1. Start **Windows Server Backup** in **Administrative Tools**.

2. On the **Actions** menu, click on **Recover**.

3. Select the server from which the data needs to be recovered, and then click on **Next**.

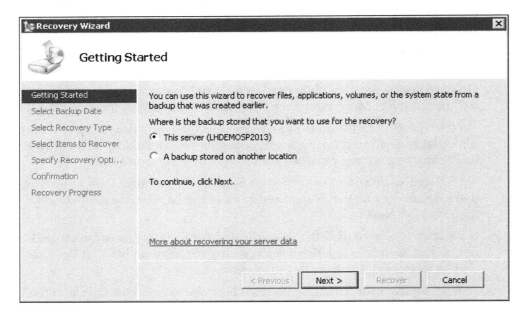

4. Select the date and time for which the restore is required, and then click on **Next**.

5. Select the application's recovery type, and then click on **Next**.

6. Navigate to **Hyper-V**, and then click on **Next**.

7. Select the restore location, and then click on **Next**.

8. Click on **Recover** to start the restore process.

Windows Server 2012 and Windows Hyper-V Server 2012

Windows Server Backup only supports recovery of backups that were made by it. Make sure that there is an access to these backups before commencing.

Use the following steps to recover from a backup containing virtual machines and the host components using Windows Server Backup:

1. Open the **Start** menu and type wbadmin.msc to open the **Windows Server Backup** tool.

2. In the **Windows Server Backup** console, in the pane on the right-hand side, click on **Recover**.

3. In the **Recovery Wizard** window, under **Getting Started**, select **This server** if the backup is stored locally, or select **A backup stored on another location** if the backup is in a storage or network folder, as shown in the following screenshot, and then click on **Next**:

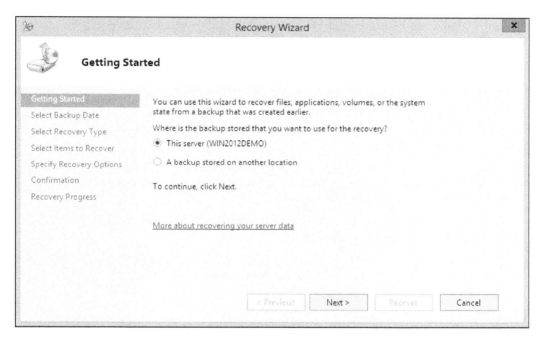

4. In the **Specify Location Type** window, select from the options **Local drives** or `Remote shared` folder. Select the option where the backup files are situated, and then click on **Next**.

5. In the **Select Backup Location** window, click on the drop-down list to select the backup location where the files are placed, and then click on **Next**.

6. In the **Select Server** window, select the server to restore data, and then click on **Next**.

7. In **Select Backup Date**, select the month, day, and time for restoring.

 To check the content of the backup, click on the hyperlink in front of the **Recoverable** items, and then click on **Next** when done.

8. On the **Select Recovery Type** page, select what needs to be recovered.

9. It is possible to choose from the following options: **Files and folders, Hyper-V, Volumes, Applications**, and **System State**. To recover the virtual machine and host components, select **Hyper-V** and then click on **Next**.

10. On the **Select Items to Recover** page, select the virtual machine. If Hyper-V settings need to be recovered, select the **Host Component** option, and then click on **Next**.

11. In the **Specify Recovery** options, select from the following options: **Recover to original location, Recover to alternate location**, and **copy to folder**. Select the option that suits the environment, and then click on **Next**.

12. In the **Confirmation** window, verify the recovery items that will be restored and then click on **Recover**.

13. Wait until the restore is complete and then click on **Close** to close **Recovery Wizard**.

14. To check the recovered items, in the **Windows Server Backup** console, under **Messages**, double-click on the **Recovery** event. The **Application recovery** window will then open.

15. To check the recovered files, click on **View list of all recovered files** in the **Application recovery** window.

16. To check whether the restoration was successful, open the **Hyper-V Manager** and check whether the restored virtual machines are listed.

Snapshots

Backups can take a very long time to complete and could affect the performance of your system given the amount of resources, such as memory and disk I/O they take while creating the actual backup. If you are backing up a live system, you could run into issues with data corruption; for example, if a user moves a file into a directory that has already been backed up, then that file would be completely missing on the backup media, since the backup operation had already taken place before the addition of the file.

For more information, see Computer data storage available at:
http://en.wikipedia.org/wiki/Computer_data_storage

In order to prevent this you could temporarily disable the write access to a database during the backup; however, doing this requires downtime which may or may not be acceptable in your environment depending upon your **service-level agreement** (**SLA**).

To avoid downtime, you may instead perform the backup using a snapshot. A snapshot is a file-based representation of the state of a virtual machine at a given time. A snapshot file includes both configuration and disk data. Administrators typically use snapshots for more repeatable kinds of backups such as those before performing:

- Software updates
- Migrations or upgrades
- Software installation and configuration
- Registry changes
- Problem troubleshooting

In Hyper-V, you take a snapshot of a virtual server by opening **Hyper-V Manager** by right-clicking on the virtual server, and then clicking on **Snapshot,** or by clicking on **Snapshot** in the pane on the right-hand side of the screen. The snapshot is then saved to the disk as an **Automatic Virtual Hard Disk** (**AVHD**) file and stored within the virtual server folder on the Hyper-V server. If you need to revert back to when the snapshot was taken, use the **Revert** option in Hyper-V Manager by right-clicking on the selected snapshot, and then clicking on **Revert** or by clicking on **Revert** in the pane on the right-hand side of the screen.

Failover clustering

Windows Server 2008, Windows Server 2008 R2, and Windows Server 2012 provide the failover clustering feature, which allows you to put roles or Hyper-V virtual servers into a high-availability solution.

When failover clustering is installed and configured, it uses the **Failover Cluster Management** tools to bring clustering components, such as storage, network, roles, and nodes, together into a single console.

In order to create a failover cluster that uses your Hyper-V virtual server you need to create a new cluster in the Failover Cluster Manager. To create a new cluster that includes your Hyper-V virtual servers, you can use the **Create New Cluster** wizard. Within the wizard, you can add a virtual server to your cluster by right-clicking on **Roles**, selecting **Virtual Machines**, and then clicking on **New Virtual Machine**. Select the node you want to create the new virtual machine in, follow the wizard, and then click on **Finish**.

VMware vSphere 5

VMware vSphere 5 is easily the most widely-used virtualization platform today. It is well tested and has been used in virtualizing SharePoint environments ranging from very small, localized installations with just a handful of servers to exceptionally large server farms in major corporations.

An add-on product to vSphere 5 called **vSphere Data Protection (VDP)** provides fast agent-less, image-level backup and recovery, leveraging industry-leading de-duplication technology to minimize the backup infrastructure requirements and simplify management.

Although there are other tools that provide backup and restore solutions for vSphere 5, we will focus on backup and restore using VMware VDP. The steps to back up are mentioned in the following section.

Backup

1. To get started, open **vSphere Web Client** and go to the home screen.
2. For the **vSphere Data Protection (VDP)** option, click on the **Getting Started** tab.

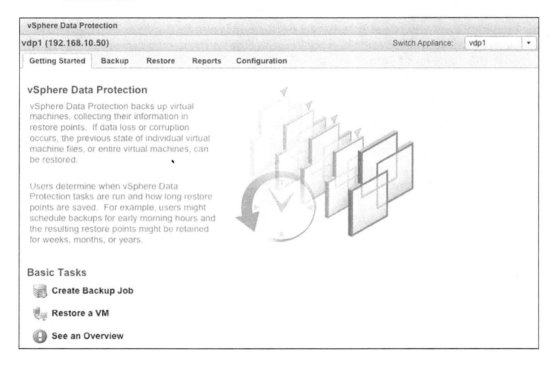

3. Under **Basic Tasks**, click on **Create Backup Job** to bring up the **New Backup Job** wizard.

4. Select the virtual machines that need to be backed up. It is possible to back up for all vSphere VMs that are managed by a single vCenter server, a single cluster, or a virtual machine, and then click on **Next**.

5. Create a schedule by specifying when the backups occur, such as daily, weekly, or on a certain day of the month (such as the first Sunday), and then click on **Next**.

6. Specify the retention policy which will determine how long the VM backup data will be stored in the backup repository, and then click on **Next**.

7. Select a name for the backup job and then click on **Next**.

8. The backups will start immediately upon submitting the new backup job (assuming there isn't resource contention, as VDP will wait until resources are available).

9. The summary status of the backup job will be available under the **Backup** tab.

10. A much more detailed backup job status can be found on the **Reports** tab, where there is information about the status of each virtual machine and its backup status. Additionally, the status of the backup repository (percent used) is visible, along with the number of successful failed backups.

Restore

With virtual machines successfully backed up, use the following steps for recovering/restoring a virtual machine using vSphere Data Protection (VDP). The steps to restore are:

1. To get started, open **vSphere Web Client** and go to the home screen.

2. Select the option to go into **vSphere Data Protection (VDP)**.

3. Click on the **Restore** tab. There is a list of all the successful virtual machine backups with multiple backup points of each VM (assuming multiple backups have occurred).

4. To recover from a backup, simply select the checkbox next to the VM backup point that needs to be recovered, and then click on **Restore**.

 If many changes have not occurred to the VM disk file since the backup, only changed blocks will be restored and recovery can be done in seconds.

If only the restore of specific files from a virtual machine backup is required, use vSphere Data Protection Restore Client. It allows mounting of specific virtual machine backups as file systems and then browsing through the file system to find the files that need to be restored.

Snapshots

Like Hyper-V, vSphere supports snapshots. To create a snapshot in the vSphere client, select **Inventory**, and then click on **Virtual Machine** and select the virtual machine you wish to take a snapshot of. Click on **Snapshot**, and then click on **Take Snapshot**. Provide a name and description for the snapshot, optionally select the **Snapshot the virtual machine's memory** checkbox to capture the memory of the virtual machine. You can optionally select the **Quiesce guest file system (Needs VMware Tools installed)** checkbox to pause running processes on the guest operating system so that file system contents are in a known consistent state when you take the snapshot, and then click on **Ok**.

In order to revert to a snapshot in the vSphere client, you can right-click a virtual machine in the vSphere client inventory and select **Revert to Current Snapshot**. The virtual machine power and data states are returned to the states they were in at the time you took the parent snapshot. If the parent snapshot is a memory snapshot, the virtual machine is restored to an on-power state.

Failover clustering

In addition to Hyper-V virtual machines, Windows Server 2008, Windows Server 2008 R2, and Windows Server 2012 support failover clustering for vSphere virtual machines. When creating a cluster using the Failover Cluster Manager, you can select vSphere virtual machines to add to your clustering nodes.

For more information, see the *Setup for Failover Clustering and Microsoft Cluster Service* guide for ESXi 5.x available at:

http://pubs.vmware.com/vsphere-51/topic/com.vmware.
ICbase/PDF/vsphere-esxi-vcenter-server-511-setup-
mscs.pdf

Summary

This chapter wraps up the backup and restore approaches for a complete SharePoint environment. Yes, it is complicated and not something that can be done in an afternoon. It is not just the planning and testing that was discussed in the previous chapter, but the understanding of the SharePoint infrastructure.

From reading this and the previous chapter, it can be seen that the skillset that is needed is not just SharePoint, but rather the Microsoft server stack.

The next chapter introduces you to SharePoint out-of-the-box DR processes through SharePoint's Central Administration interface. Both this chapter and the next should be compared together so that you truly understand the DR process for SharePoint.

5
Central Administration and Other Native Backup and Restore Options

While SharePoint technologies have always provided methods for backing up and restoring data, the scope and capabilities have changed with each SharePoint generation. From the `owsadm.exe` command line tool in the original SharePoint Team Services (first generation), to unattached content database restores in SharePoint 2010 (fourth generation), backup and restore capabilities have significantly evolved and improved.

This chapter introduces you to native backup and restore options, and how to perform them using the Central Administration console and Windows PowerShell. Although the STSADM command line tool is still included for compatibility support to older versions, it is a deprecated utility, replaced and magnified by PowerShell, and is only referenced in this chapter for completeness.

Generally speaking, SharePoint 2013 backup and recovery operates around the following four primary native options:

- Farm recovery using a farm backup created with built-in tools
- Component recovery using the farm backup system
- Data recovery from an unattached content database
- Site collection recovery from a site collection backup

Do not fool yourself; backup and restore is a very complex topic due to the nature of SharePoint. SharePoint as a platform has a variety of components and moving parts. It is very important that you have thorough understanding of what you can and cannot accomplish natively, so you know where you may need to augment your environment in order to achieve the outcome you are looking for. The goal of this chapter is to present you with the building blocks necessary for you to start thinking about how you are going to implement your DR strategy. This chapter is not intended to be exhaustive or comprehensive (Microsoft TechNet is there for that), but is intended to give you the foundational knowledge you need in order to make the right decisions regarding when, where, and what tools you can use, and how to avoid the potential shortcomings of each.

In this chapter, we will cover the following topics:

- Farm backup and restore
- Farm configuration backup and restore
- Web application backup and restore
- Service application backup and restore
- Content database backup and restore
- Customizations backup and restore
- Site collections backup and restore
- Apps backup and restore
- Sites, lists, and libraries – backup and restore
- SharePoint templates

Farm backup and restore

A complete SharePoint farm backup will consist of both the configuration and the content. This is a backup of the entire SharePoint environment that is intended to mitigate the possibility of data loss occurring from hardware failures, power outages, environmental disasters, and so on. This level of backup can be performed through the Central Administration GUI, Windows PowerShell, and by using STSADM. Please note that, if you are performing this backup for the first time, you must perform a full backup before you can perform a differential one.

Back up using the Central Administration GUI

To back up a farm by using the Central Administration website, perform the following procedure:

1. Verify that the user account you are using to perform this operation. The user account performing the procedure must be a member of the Farm Administrators group in the SharePoint farm.

2. Create a network folder where you can store your backup files. The server farm user account you just verified as a Farm Administrator, the Windows SharePoint Services Timer V4 service account, and also the SQL Server services account, must have Full Control permissions to this folder.

3. Open up the **Central Administration** home page, look in the **Backup and Restore** section, and click on **Perform a backup**, as shown in the following screenshot:

4. On the **Perform a Backup - Step 1 of 2: Select Component to back up** page, select the checkbox next to **Farm**, and then click on **Next** as shown in the following screenshot:

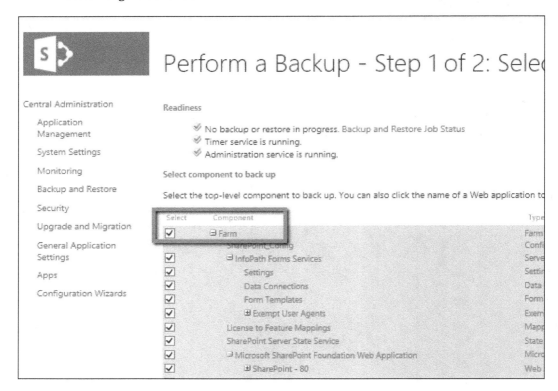

5. On the **Start Backup - Step 2 of 2: Select Backup Options** page, in the **Backup Type** section, select the **Full** radio button, as shown in the following screenshot:

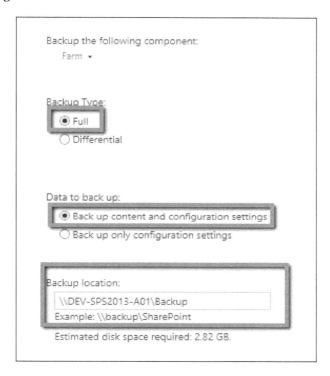

6. In the **Data to back up** section, select the **Back up content and configuration settings** radio button, as highlighted in the previous screenshot.

7. In the **Backup location** section, enter the **Universal Naming Convention (UNC)** path of the backup folder (for example, \\DEV-SPS2013-A01\Backup), and then click on **Start Backup**.

Back up using PowerShell

To back up a farm by using Windows PowerShell, perform the following procedure:

1. Verify that the user account you are using to perform this operation. The account must have the *securityadmin* fixed server role on the SQL Server instance, the *db_owner database* role on all the databases that will be interacted with, and must be a member of the Administrators group on the server where you are running the cmdlets.

2. Create a network folder where you can store your backup files. The Administrator account, the Windows SharePoint Services Timer V4 service account, and also the SQL Server services account, must have Full Control permissions to this folder.

3. Open the SharePoint 2013 Management Shell (as an Administrator).

4. Type the following command (shown in cmdlet syntax) to perform the backup:

```
Backup-SPFarm -Directory <BackupFolder> -BackupMethod {Full |
Differential} [-Verbose]
```

A real world example will look as shown in the following command:

```
Backup-SPFarm -Directory \\DEV-SPS2013-A01\Backup -BackupMethod
Full
```

Restore using the Central Administration GUI

To restore a by farm using the Central Administration website, perform the following procedure:

1. Verify that the user account you are using to perform this operation. The account must be a member of the Farm Administrators group in the SharePoint farm.

2. The server farm user account you just verified as a Farm Administrator, the Windows SharePoint Services Timer V4 service account, and also the SQL Server services account, must have Full Control permissions on the network folder where you are storing your backup files.

3. Open up the **Central Administration** home page, look in the **Backup and Restore** section, and click on **Restore from a backup**, as highlighted in the following screenshot:

4. On the **Backup and Restore History** page, select the backup job that contains the **Farm** backup, and then click on **Next,** as shown in the following screenshot:

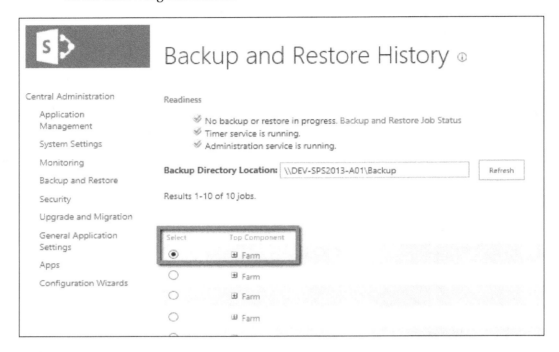

5. On the **Restore from Backup - Step 2 of 3: Select Component to Restore** page, select the checkbox next to **Farm**, and then click on **Next,** as shown in the following screenshot:

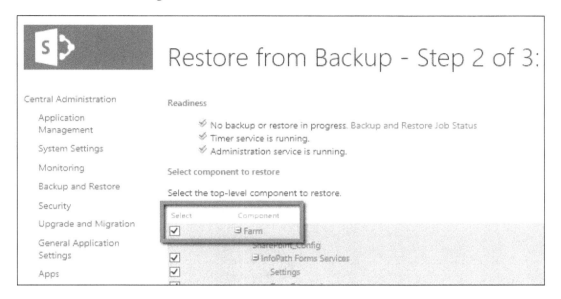

6. On the **Restore from Backup - Step 3 of 3: Select Restore Options** page, in the **Restore Component** section, make sure that **Farm** appears in the list. Then, in the **Restore Only Configuration Settings** section, make sure that the **Restore content and configuration settings** radio button is selected. Next, in the **Restore Options** section, under **Type of restore**, select the **Same configuration** radio button, as shown here:

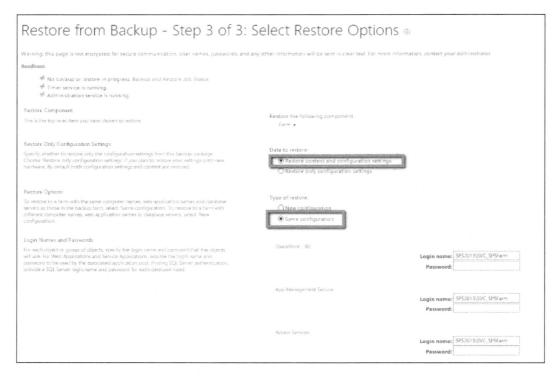

7. Next, in the **Login Names and Passwords** section, type the passwords for all of the listed logins. Click on **Start Restore**.

8. Once the restore process completes, you will likely need to restart one or more service applications. Go to the Manage services on server page and start any services related to the service applications that should be running. Do this by clicking on Start in the Actions column next to the specific service application.

Restore using PowerShell

To restore a farm by using Windows PowerShell, perform the following procedure:

1. Verify that the user account you are using to perform this operation has the securityadmin fixed server role on the SQL Server instance, the db_owner database role on all the databases that will be interacted with, and is a member of the Administrators group on the server where you are running the cmdlets.

2. The Farm Administrator account, the Windows SharePoint Services Timer V4 service account, and also the SQL Server services account, must have Full Control permissions on the network folder where you are storing your backup files.

3. Open the SharePoint 2013 Management Shell (as an Administrator).

4. Type the following command (shown in cmdlet syntax) to perform the restore:

    ```
    Restore-SPFarm -Directory <BackupFolder> -RestoreMethod Overwrite
    [-BackupId <GUID>]
    ```

    A real world example will look as shown in the following command:

    ```
    Restore-SPFarm -Directory \\DEV-SPS2013-A01\Backup -RestoreMethod
    Overwrite
    ```

5. Next, type the following command (shown in cmdlet syntax) to start the necessary service applications, cmdlet syntax:

    ```
    Start-SPServiceInstance -Identity <ServiceApplicationID>
    ```

    A real world example will look as shown in the following command:

    ```
    Start-SPServiceInstance 67877d63-bff4-4521-867a-ef4979ba07ce
    ```

> To get a list of available services, you can use the Get-SPServiceInstance cmdlet:
>
> ```
> Get-SPServiceInstance | Select TypeName, ID, Status
> ```
>
> For more information about this cmdlet and its syntax, visit http://technet.microsoft.com/en-us/library/ff607570.aspx.

Caveats and considerations

The following are caveats and considerations that should be understood:

- **SharePoint version and topology constraints**: You cannot back up from one version and restore to another (for example, from SharePoint 2010 Foundation to SharePoint 2013 Foundation), nor between editions (for example, from SharePoint 2013 Foundation to SharePoint 2013 Server). You cannot perform backups/restores using different service pack levels. You also cannot back up a standalone farm and restore it to a multi-server farm, or vice-versa.

- **Farm performance**: Backing up the farm will affect farm performance while the backup is running. Consider scheduling during off-peak times.

- **Certificates**: Certificates that you use to form trust relationships with other farms will not be backed up. Ensure that you have copies, as the trust relationships will need to be recreated. For more information, visit `http:// technet.microsoft.com/en-us/library/ee704552.aspx`.

- **Web.config files**: Manual changes to the `Web.config` file (safe controls, HTTP modules, and so on) will not be preserved and can be overwritten the next time that web application provisioning occurs. Changes to `Web.config` made via Central Administration or the SharePoint 2013 API and object model will be stored in the configuration database and can be recovered through farm or configuration backups. Changes made to `Web.config` outside of these methods will not be stored in the configuration database, and will need to be protected by using file system backups. A special consideration is the `Web.config` file for forms-based authentication, which is manually edited and must be backed up using a file system backup.

- **Configuration database**: In previous iterations of SharePoint, the configuration database could not be restored. In SharePoint 2013, you can restore the farm configuration directly without having to restore the configuration database.

- **Content databases**: The **identifier (ID)** of each content database is retained when you restore or reattach a database.

- **Business data connectivity service**: A farm backup will back up external content type definitions, but not the corresponding data source. This needs to be backed up and restored independently.

- **Service applications**: The restore process will not automatically start all of the service applications; you must manually start them using either Central Administration or Windows PowerShell.

- **Binary Large Objects (BLOBs)**: SharePoint only backs up remote BLOBs only if you are using FILESTREAM, BLOBs using any other providers will need to be manually backed up. This will require significant planning to ensure that metadata between BLOBs and content databases is kept in sync.

- **Transparent Data Encryption (TDE)**: If your environment uses TDE, the TDE encryption key will not be backed up or restored; this must be done manually. For more information, visit `http://technet.microsoft.com/en-us/library/bb934049.aspx`.

- **Offline content**: If content is taken off-line for editing, once the content is restored, the server will automatically synchronize the off-line content which could result in data loss on the user's copies of the material.

- **Claims-based authentication**: Duplicate or additional claims providers are often visible for restored web applications configured for claims-based authentication. For more information, visit `http://technet.microsoft.com/en-us/library/ee748647.aspx`.

- **Items not included**: The following list includes settings not included in a farm backup that are stored on the web servers:

    ° Application pool account passwords
    ° HTTP compression settings
    ° Time-out settings
    ° Custom ISAPI filters
    ° Computer domain memberships
    ° IPsec settings
    ° NLB settings
    ° SSL certificates and IP addressing
    ° Manual `Web.config` changes
    ° Additional files in the features directories that were not installed through solutions
    ° Files manually added to the **global assembly cache (GAC)**

Farm configuration backup and restore

A farm configuration backup will back up the configuration data from a configuration database, including settings for information rights management, email, anti-virus, and so on. This is only farm-level configuration and is intended to handle failures that involve the configuration database, but not other SharePoint components.

Appropriate use cases include replicating a standardized farm configuration and moving configurations between environments. When using the Central Administration GUI, you can only back up the local configuration database (local to the farm whose Central Administration website you are on). With Windows PowerShell, you can back up any configuration database on the local farm, on a remote farm, or from an unattached configuration database (one not associated with any farm).

Back up using the Central Administration GUI

To backup a farm configuration by using the Central Administration website, perform the following procedure:

1. Verify the user account requirements. Follow the procedure in the section titled **Farm Backup and Restore,** or visit TechNet at http://technet. microsoft.com/en-us/library/ee748614.aspx.

2. Open up the **Central Administration** home page, look in the **Backup and Restore** section, and click on **Perform a backup.**

3. On the **Perform a Backup - Step 1 of 2: Select Component to Back up** page, select the checkbox next to **Farm,** and then click on **Next.**

4. On the **Start Backup - Step 2 of 2: Select Backup Options** page, in the **Backup Type** section, select the **Full** radio button.

5. In the **Back up Only Configuration Settings** section, select the **Back up only configuration settings** radio button.

6. In the **Backup File Location** section, type the UNC path of the backup folder (for example, \\DEV-SPS2013-A01\Backup), and then click on **Start Backup.**

Back up using PowerShell

To back up a farm configuration using Windows PowerShell, perform the following procedure:

1. Verify the user account requirements. Follow the procedure in the section titled **Farm Backup and Restore**, or visit TechNet at http://technet. microsoft.com/en-us/library/ee748614.aspx.

2. Open the SharePoint 2013 Management Shell (as an Administrator).

3. Type the following command (shown in cmdlet syntax) to perform the backup:

```
Backup-SPConfigurationDatabase -Directory <BackupFolder>
[-DatabaseServer <DatabaseServerName> -DatabaseName <DatabaseName>
-DatabaseCredentials <WindowsPowerShellCredentialObject>]
```

A real world example will look as shown in the following command:

```
Backup-SPConfigurationDatabase -Directory \\DEV-SPS2013-A01\Backup
-DatabaseServer DEV-SPS2013-A01
```

Restore using the Central Administration GUI

To restore a farm configuration by using the Central Administration website, perform the following procedure:

1. Verify the user account requirements. Follow the procedure in the section titled **Farm Backup and Restore**, or visit TechNet at http://technet. microsoft.com/en-us/library/ee748614.aspx.

2. Open up the **Central Administration** homepage, look in the **Backup and Restore** section, and click on **Restore from a backup**.

3. On the **Backup and Restore History** page, select the backup job that contains the farm backup, and then click on **Next**.

4. On the **Restore from Backup - Step 2 of 3: Select Component to Restore** page, select the checkbox next to **Farm**, and then click on **Next**.

5. On the **Restore from Backup - Step 3 of 3: Select Restore Options** page, in the **Restore Component** section, make sure that **Farm** appears in the list. Next, in the **Restore Only Configuration Settings** section, make sure the **Restore only configuration settings** radio button is selected. Next, in the **Restore Options** section, select the **Same configuration** radio button. Next, in the **Login Names and Passwords** section, type all the passwords for all the listed logins. Click on **Start Restore**.

6. Once the restore process completes, you will likely need to restart one or more service applications. Go to the **Manage services on server** page and start any services related to service applications that should be running. Do this by clicking on **Start** in the **Actions** column next to the specific service application.

Restore using PowerShell

To restore a farm configuration by using Windows PowerShell, perform the following procedure:

1. Verify the user account requirements. Follow the procedure in the section titled **Farm Backup and Restore**, or visit TechNet at `http://technet.microsoft.com/en-us/library/ee748614.aspx`.

2. Open the SharePoint 2013 Management Shell (as an Administrator).

3. Type the following command (shown in cmdlet syntax) to perform the restore:

```
Restore-SPFarm -Directory <RestoreShare> -RestoreMethod Overwrite
-ConfigurationOnly
```

A real world example will look as shown in the following command:

```
Restore-SPFarm -Directory \\DEV-SPS2013-A01\Backup -RestoreMethod
Overwrite -ConfigurationOnly
```

Caveats and considerations

The following are caveats and considerations that should be understood:

- **Web applications**: Farm configuration backups do not include any web application settings.

- **Service applications**: Farm configuration backup does not include any information related to service applications. In order to recover service applications, you must pursue alternative methods. For more information, visit `http://technet.microsoft.com/en-us/library/ee428318.aspx`.

- **Limited tools**: You cannot use SQL Server tools or Microsoft Data Protection Manager to back up the farm configuration.

- **Restore behavior**: A farm configuration restore will overwrite any settings in the farm that have values that are set within the configuration-only backup.

Web application backup and restore

A web application backup will include the IIS settings (that exist inside Office SharePoint Server) and all content databases that are associated with the web application. This is a more granular backup than the entire farm, but is recommended in addition to regular backups at the farm level. Web application backups can be performed through the Central Administration GUI, Windows PowerShell, and using STSADM. Note that if you are performing this backup for the first time, you must perform a Full backup before you can perform Differential one.

Back up using the Central Administration GUI

To back up a web application by using the Central Administration website, perform the following procedure:

1. Verify user account requirements. Follow the procedure in the section titled **Farm Backup and Restore**, or visit TechNet at `http://technet.microsoft. com/en-us/library/ee748614.aspx`.

2. Open up the Central Administration homepage, look in the **Backup and Restore** section, and click on **Perform a backup**.

3. On the **Perform a Backup - Step 1 of 2: Select Component to Back Up** page, select the web application from the list of components, and then click on **Next**.

4. On the **Perform a Backup - Step 2 of 2: Select Backup Options** page, in the **Backup Type** section, select either the **Full** radio button or the **Differential** radio button.

5. In the **Backup File Location** section, enter the UNC path of the backup folder (for example, `\\DEV-SPS2013-A01\Backup`), and then click on **Start Backup**.

Back up using PowerShell

To back up a web application by using Windows PowerShell, perform the following procedure:

1. Verify the user account requirements. Follow the procedure in the section titled **Farm Backup and Restore**, or visit TechNet at `http://technet. microsoft.com/en-us/library/ee748614.aspx`.

2. Open the SharePoint 2013 Management Shell (as an Administrator).

3. Type the following command (shown in cmdlet syntax) to perform the backup:

```
Backup-SPFarm -Directory <BackupFolder> -BackupMethod {Full |
Differential} -Item <WebApplicationName> [-Verbose]
```

A real world example will look as shown in the following example:

```
Backup-SPFarm -Directory \\DEV-SPS2013-A01\Backup -BackupMethod
Full -Item "SharePoint - 80"
```

Restore using the Central Administration GUI

To restore a web application by using the Central Administration website, perform the following procedure:

1. Verify the user account requirements. Follow the procedure in the section titled **Farm Backup and Restore**, or visit TechNet at http:// technet.microsoft.com/en-us/library/ee748614.aspx.

2. Open up the **Central Administration** home page, look in the **Backup and Restore** section, and click on **Restore from a Backup**.

3. On the **Backup and Restore History** page, select the backup job that contains the web application backup, and then click on **Next**.

4. On the **Restore from Backup - Step 2 of 3: Select Component to Restore** page, select the web application, and then click on **Next**.

5. On the **Restore from a Backup - Step 3 of 3: Select Restore Options** page, in the **Restore Component** section, make sure that **Farm\<Web Application>** appears in the **Restore the following content** list.

6. In the **Restore Options** section, under **Type of Restore**, select the **Same configuration option**. Verify the login name and the password, and then click on **Start Restore**.

Restore using PowerShell

To restore a web application by using Windows PowerShell, do the following:

1. Verify the user account requirements. Follow the procedure in the section titled **Farm Backup and Restore**, or visit TechNet at http://technet. microsoft.com/en-us/library/ee748614.aspx.

2. Open the SharePoint 2013 Management Shell (as an Administrator).

3. Type the following command (shown in cmdlet syntax) to perform the restore:

```
Restore-SPFarm -Directory <BackupFolderName> -RestoreMethod
Overwrite -Item <WebApplicationName> [-BackupId <GUID>] [-Verbose]
```

A real world example will look as shown in the following command:

```
Restore-SPFarm -Directory \\DEV-SPS2013-A01\Backup -RestoreMethod
Overwrite -Item "SharePoint - 80"
```

Caveats and considerations

The following are caveats and considerations that should be understood:

- **Limited parallelism**: Unless you are doing a full farm backup/restore, you can only do one web application backup/restore at a time when using the built-in tools.

- **Farm performance**: Backing up the web application will affect farm performance while the backup is running. Consider scheduling during off-peak times.

- **Restore behavior**: A farm configuration restore will overwrite any settings in the farm that have values that are set within the configuration-only backup.

- **Object cache**: If you are using the object cache, the object cache user accounts will need to be manually configured post-restore.

- **Web.config files**: Manual changes to the `Web.config` file (safe controls, HTTP modules, and so on) will not be preserved and can be overwritten the next time web application provisioning occurs. Changes to `Web.config` made via Central Administration or the SharePoint 2013 API and object model will be stored in the configuration database and can be recovered through farm or configuration backups. Changes made to `Web.config` outside of these methods will not be stored in the configuration database, and will need to be protected using file system backups. A special consideration is the `Web.config` file for forms-based authentication, which is manually edited and must be backed up using a file system backup.

- **Claims-based authentication**: Duplicate or additional claims providers are often visible for restored web applications configured for claims-based authentication. For more information, visit `http://technet.microsoft.com/en-us/library/ee748647.aspx`.

Service application backup and restore

A service application backup will include all service application-related data and configurations that are associated with that specific service application. This option is intended for situations where you may need to restore a specific service application only, rather than having to restore the entire farm. Service application backups can be performed through the Central Administration GUI, Windows PowerShell, and by using STSADM. Please note that if you are performing this backup for the first time, you must perform a Full backup before you can perform a Differential one.

Back up using the Central Administration GUI

To back up a service application by using the Central Administration website, perform the following procedure:

1. Verify the user account requirements. Follow the procedure in the section titled **Farm Backup and Restore**, or visit TechNet at `http://technet.microsoft.com/en-us/library/ee748614.aspx`.

2. Open up the **Central Administration** homepage, look in the **Backup and Restore** section, and click on **Perform a backup**.

3. On the **Perform a Backup - Step 1 of 2: Select Component to Back Up** page, select the service application from the list of components, and then click on **Next**.

4. On the **Start Backup - Step 2 of 2: Select Backup Options** page, in the **Backup Type** section, select either the **Full** or **Differential** radio buttons.

5. In the **Backup File Location** section, type the UNC path of the backup folder (for example, `\\DEV-SPS2013-A01\Backup`), and then click on **Start Backup**.

Back up using PowerShell

To back up a service application by using Windows PowerShell, perform the following procedure:

1. Verify the user account requirements. Follow the procedure in the section titled **Farm Backup and Restore**, or visit TechNet at `http://technet.microsoft.com/en-us/library/ee748614.aspx`.

2. Open the SharePoint 2013 Management Shell (as an Administrator).

3. Type the following command (shown in cmdlet syntax) to perform the backup:

```
Backup-SPFarm -Directory <BackupFolder> -BackupMethod {Full |
Differential} -Item <ServiceApplicationName>  [-Verbose]
```

A real world example will look as shown in the following code:

```
Backup-SPFarm -Directory \\DEV-SPS2013-A01\Backup -BackupMethod
Full -Item "Farm\Shared Services\Shared Services Applications\
Access Services"
```

You can list all of the components that will be backed up without actually performing a backup. To list the components, use the ShowTree parameter, which is shown in cmdlet syntax, below:

Backup-SPFarm –ShowTree -Item <item> -Verbose

A real world example will look as shown in the following code:

Backup-SPFarm –ShowTree -Item "Microsoft SharePoint Foundation Web Application" -Verbose

For more information about this cmdlet and its syntax, visit `http://technet.microsoft.com/en-us/library/ff607881.aspx`.

Restore using the Central Administration GUI

To restore a service application by using the Central Administration website, perform the following procedure:

1. Verify the user account requirements. Follow the procedure in the section titled **Farm Backup and Restore**, or visit TechNet at `http://technet.microsoft.com/en-us/library/ee748614.aspx`.

2. Open up the **Central Administration** home page, look in the **Backup and Restore** section, and click on **Restore from a Backup**.

3. On the **Backup and Restore History** page, select the backup job that contains the service application backup, and then click on **Next**.

4. On the **Restore from a Backup - Step 2 of 3: Select Component to Restore** page, expand **Shared Services Applications**, select the checkbox next to the service application that you backed up, and then click on **Next**.

5. On the **Restore from a Backup - Step 3 of 3: Select Restore Options page**, in the **Restore Component** section, make sure that **Farm\Shared Services Applications\<Service application>** appears in the **Restore the following components** list.

6. In the **Restore Options** section, under **Type of Restore**, select the option that states **Same configuration**. Verify the login name and the password, and then click on **Start Restore**.

Restore using PowerShell

To restore a service application by using Windows PowerShell, perform the following procedure:

1. Verify the user account requirements. Follow the procedure in the section titled **Farm Backup and Restore,** or visit TechNet at http://technet. microsoft.com/en-us/library/ee748614.aspx.

2. Open the SharePoint 2013 Management Shell (as an Administrator).

3. Type the following command (shown in cmdlet syntax) to perform the restore:

```
Restore-SPFarm -Directory <BackupFolder> -Item
"<ServiceApplicationName>" -RestoreMethod Overwrite [-BackupId
<GUID>] [-Verbose]
```

A real world example will look as shown in the following code:

```
Restore-SPFarm -Directory \\DEV-SPS2013-A01\Backup -Item "Farm\
Shared Services\Shared Services Applications\Access Services"
-RestoreMethod Overwrite
```

Caveats and considerations

The following are caveats and considerations that should be understood:

- **Farm performance**: Backing up the farm will affect farm performance while the backup is running. Consider scheduling during off-peak times.

- **Parallelism**: You can backup/restore one service application at a time, or you can do them all together. Note that if you are consolidating the backup you will need to consider all of the implications associated with all of the different service applications simultaneously, rather than handling them individually, which introduces planning overhead and more potential for oversight.

- **External data**: External data sources, for example those potentially used with the Business Data Connectivity service application, will need to be backed up separately. In addition, if data sources are restored to a different location, the new location information must be configured in the external content type definition, or the Business Data Connectivity service will be unable to locate the data source.

- **Service application specifics**: Some service applications are exclusive, while others can be shared. Make sure that you pay attention to the service application proxy associated with your service application, and that it is also included as part of the backup.

- **Binary Large Objects (BLOBs)**: SharePoint backs up and restores remote BLOBs only if you are using FILESTREAM. BLOBs using any other providers will need to be backed up and restored independently.

- **Tool limitations**: Certain service applications can only be comprehensively backed up and restored using SharePoint 2013 native tools. These include the Business Data Connectivity, Secure Store, User Profile, Managed Metadata, and Search service applications. In these cases, you will need to back up the databases associated with the service applications by using SQL Server tools. You will need to use SQL Server tools to restore the databases associated with these service applications.

- **Specific service applications additional steps**: While the process detailed in this section is applicable to most service applications, specific service applications, including the User Profile service application, the Search service application, and the Secure Store Service application, require additional steps. Please visit the Microsoft Technet website for additional technical details. Links for these have been provided as follows:

    ° *User Profile backup*: http://technet.microsoft.com/en-us/library/gg576965.aspx

    ° *User Profile restore*: http://technet.microsoft.com/en-us/library/gg985419.aspx

    ° *Search backup*: http://technet.microsoft.com/en-us/library/ee748635.aspx

    ° *Search restore*: http://technet.microsoft.com/en-us/library/ee748654.aspx

    ° *Secure Store backup*: http://technet.microsoft.com/en-us/library/ee748648.aspx

    ° *Secure Store restore*: http://technet.microsoft.com/en-us/library/ee748602.aspx

Content database backup and restore

Content databases tend to grow at a higher rate than other farm databases, and they are typically backed up separately from farm backups. Content database backups and restores can be performed by using any of the built-in tools. With SQL Server tools, you also have the ability to back up databases to snapshots. With PowerShell, you also have the ability to attach and restore read-only databases. You can also restore content from an unattached content database in SharePoint 2013, which includes granularly restoring sites, site collections, lists, and document libraries without having to attach the content database to the farm.

Back up using the Central Administration GUI

To back up a content database by using the Central Administration website, perform the following procedure:

1. Verify the user account requirements. Follow the procedure in the section titled **Farm Backup and Restore**, or visit TechNet at `http://technet.microsoft.com/en-us/library/ee748614.aspx`.

2. Open up the **Central Administration** homepage, look in the **Backup and Restore** section, and click on **Perform a backup**.

3. On the **Perform a Backup - Step 1 of 2: Select Component to Back Up** page, select the content database from the list of components, and then click on **Next**.

4. On the **Start Backup - Step 2 of 2: Select Backup Options** page, in the **Backup Type** section, select either the **Full** radio button or the **Differential** radio button.

5. In the **Backup File Location** section, enter the UNC path of the backup folder (for example, `\\DEV-SPS2013-A01\Backup`), and then click on **Start Backup**.

Back up using PowerShell

To back up a content database by using Windows PowerShell, perform the following procedure:

1. Verify the user account requirements. Follow the procedure in the section titled **Farm Backup and Restore**, or visit TechNet at `http://technet.microsoft.com/en-us/library/ee748614.aspx`.

2. Open the SharePoint 2013 Management Shell (as an Administrator).

3. Type the following command (shown in cmdlet syntax) to perform the backup:

```
Backup-SPFarm -Directory <BackupFolder> -BackupMethod {Full |
Differential} -Item <ContentDatabaseName> [-Verbose]
```

A real world example will look as shown in the following code:

```
Backup-SPFarm -Directory \\DEV-SPS2013-A01\Backup -BackupMethod
Full -Item WSS_Content
```

To list all of the content databases that belong to the SharePoint farm, use the `Get-SPContentDatabase` cmdlet; and a real world example is shown as follows:

```
Get-SPContentDatabase
```

For more information about this cmdlet and its syntax, visit `http://technet.microsoft.com/en-us/library/ff607828.aspx`.

Restore using the Central Administration GUI

To restore a content database by using the Central Administration website, perform the following procedure:

1. Verify the user account requirements. Follow the procedure in the section titled **Farm Backup and Restore**, or visit TechNet at `http://technet.microsoft.com/en-us/library/ee748614.aspx`.

2. Open up the **Central Administration** home page, look in the **Backup and Restore** section, and click on **Restore from a backup**.

3. On the **Backup and Restore History** page, select the backup job that contains the content database backup, and then click on **Next**.

4. On the **Restore from a Backup - Step 2 of 3: Select Component to Restore** page, select the checkbox next to the content database that you backed up, and then click on **Next**.

5. On the **Restore from a Backup - Step 3 of 3: Select Restore Options** page, in the **Restore Options** section, under **Type of Restore**, select the option that states **Same configuration**, and then click on **Start Restore**.

Restore using PowerShell

To restore a content database by using Windows PowerShell, perform the following procedure:

1. Verify the user account requirements. Follow the procedure in the section titled **Farm Backup and Restore**, or visit TechNet at `http://technet.microsoft.com/en-us/library/ee748614.aspx`.

2. Open the SharePoint 2013 Management Shell (as an Administrator).

3. Type the following command (shown in cmdlet syntax) to perform the restore:

```
Restore-SPFarm -Directory <BackupFolder> -RestoreMethod Overwrite
-Item <ContentDatabase> [-BackupId <GUID>] [-Verbose]
```

A real world example will look as shown in the following command:

```
Restore-SPFarm -Directory \\DEV-SPS2013-A01\Backup -Item WSS_
Content -RestoreMethod Overwrite
```

With PowerShell, you can also attach and restore a read-only content database by performing the following procedure:

1. Open the SharePoint 2013 Management Shell (as an Administrator).

2. Type the following command (shown in cmdlet syntax) to perform the restore:

```
Mount-SPContentDatabase -Name <DatabaseName> -WebApplication
<WebApplicationID> [-Verbose]
```

A real world example will look as shown in the following command:

```
Mount-SPContentDatabase -Name "WSS_Content" -WebApplication
http://dev-sps2013-a01:8080
```

Restore using unattached content databases

You can also restore content from an unattached content database. However, this is a multi-step procedure. Using the Central Administration GUI, you first need to mount the unattached database, and backup the entire site collection, or export an individual site or list out of the desired site collection housed within that content database. Then, using PowerShell, you need to import the site collection, site, or list to an available site collection in your farm as explained in the following procedure:

1. Verify the user account you are using to perform this operation. The user account must be a member of the farm administrators group in the SharePoint farm and also a member of the db_owner fixed database role on the database being interacted with. Create a network folder where you want to store your backup files. The farm administrator, the Windows SharePoint Services Timer V4 service account, and also the SQL Server services account must have Full Control permissions to the folder storing your backups.

2. Open up the **Central Administration** home page, click on **Backup and Restore**.

3. On the **Backup and Restore** page, in the **Granular Backup** section, click on **Recover data from an unattached content database**.

4. On the **Unattached Content Database Data Recovery** page, enter the database server name into the **Database Server** text box and enter the database name into the **Database Name** text box. Then select the database authentication method that you want to use.

5. Select the **Browse content** radio button, click on **Next**, and then click on **Start Restore**.

6. On the **Browse content** page, select the site collection, site, or list that you want to restore, then select either the **Backup site collection** option or the **Export site or list** option, and then click on **Next**.

7. In the **Backup File Location** section, enter the UNC path of the backup folder (for example, \\DEV-SPS2013-A01\Backup\DocLibraryExport.cmp), and then click on **Start Backup**.

8. Next, open the SharePoint 2013 Management Shell (as an Administrator).

9. Use the following command (shown in cmdlet syntax) to perform the restore, cmdlet syntax:

```
Import-SPWeb -Identity <SiteURL> -Path <ExportFileName> [-Force]
[-NoFileCompression] [-Verbose]
```

A real world example will look as shown in the following command:

```
Import-SPWeb -Identity http://dev-sps2013-a01/Subsite2 -Path \\
DEV-SPS2013-A01\Backup\DocLibraryExport.cmp -Force
```

Back up and restore using SQL Server tools

The following are links that explain how to backup and restore by using SQL Server tools:

- To back up a content database by using SQL Server tools, visit http://technet.microsoft.com/en-us/library/ee428327.aspx.

- To back up databases to snapshots, visit http://technet.microsoft.com/en-us/library/ee748594.aspx.

- To restore a content database by using SQL Server tools, visit http://technet.microsoft.com/en-us/library/ee748604.aspx#proc3.

Caveats and considerations

The following are caveats and considerations that should be understood:

- **Farm performance**: Backing up the content databases will affect farm performance while the backup is running. Consider scheduling during off-peak times.

- **Transparent Data Encryption (TDE)**: If your environment uses TDE, the TDE encryption key will not be backed up or restored; this must be done manually. For more information, visit http://technet.microsoft.com/en-us/library/bb934049.aspx.

- **Binary Large Objects (BLOBs)**: SharePoint backs up and restores remote BLOBs only if you are using FILESTREAM; BLOBs using any other providers will need to be backup up and restored independently.

- **Database snapshots**: Database snapshots are read-only static views of a source database as it existed at the time of snapshot creation, minus any uncommitted transactions. Transactions in the database are not affected, but uncommitted transactions are rolled back. For more information, visit http://technet. microsoft.com/en-us/library/ms175158(SQL.105).aspx.

- **Read-only databases**: When a read-only database is attached, it is automatically placed in read/write mode. Note that you can only use Windows PowerShell to attach and restore a read-only content database.

Customizations backup and restore

There are many possible customizations that you can make to your SharePoint sites, and unfortunately there is no one, definitive backup/restore process. Customizations can be developed site elements including WebParts, workflows, event receivers, timer jobs, and so on. Customizations can be authored site elements such as master pages, forms, layout pages, and so on. Customizations can also be third party products and their associated application components. Some customizations can be packaged as solutions; others may not. Each kind of customization requires a different type of backup. This section explains how to back up trusted solutions through the Central Administration GUI and Windows PowerShell. Be sure to refer to the considerations and caveats subsection for more information on the different types of customizations and recommended backups.

Back up using the Central Administration GUI

To back up a trusted solution by using the Central Administration website, perform the following procedure:

1. Verify the user account requirements. Follow the procedure in the section titled **Farm Backup and Restore**, or visit TechNet at http://technet. microsoft.com/en-us/library/ee748614.aspx.

2. Open up the **Central Administration** home page, look in the **Backup and Restore** section, and click on **Perform a backup**.

3. On the **Perform a Backup - Step 1 of 2: Select Component to Back Up** page, select **Solutions** and then click on **Next**.

4. On the **Start Backup - Step 2 of 2: Select Backup Options** page, in the **Backup Type** section, select either **Full** or **Differential**.

5. In the **Backup File Location** section, enter the UNC path of the backup folder (for example, `\\DEV-SPS2013-A01\Backup`), and then click on **Start Backup**.

Back up using PowerShell

To back up a trusted solution by using Windows PowerShell, perform the following procedure:

1. Verify the user account requirements. Follow the procedure in the section titled **Farm Backup and Restore**, or visit TechNet at `http://technet.microsoft.com/en-us/library/ee748614.aspx`.

2. Open the SharePoint 2013 Management Shell (as an Administrator).

3. Type the following command (shown in cmdlet syntax) to perform the backup:

```
Backup-SPFarm -Backupmethod full -Directory <UNC location> -Item
"farm\solutions"
```

A real world example will look as shown in the following command:

```
Backup-SPFarm -Backupmethod full -Directory \\DEV-SPS2013-A01\
Backup -Item "farm\solutions"
```

Restore using the Central Administration GUI

To restore a service application by using the Central Administration website, perform the following procedure:

1. Verify the user account requirements. Follow the procedure in the section titled **Farm Backup and Restore**, or visit TechNet at `http://technet.microsoft.com/en-us/library/ee748614.aspx`.

2. Open up the **Central Administration** home page, look in the **Backup and Restore** section, and click on **Restore from a Backup**.

3. On the **Restore from a Backup - Step 1 of 3: Select Backup to Restore** page, select the backup job that contains the trusted solution package backup, and then click on **Next**.

4. On the **Restore from a Backup - Step 2 of 3: Select Component to Restore** page, select the check box next to the solution that you backed up, and then click on **Next**.

5. On the **Restore from a Backup - Step 3 of 3: Select Restore Options** page, in the **Restore Component** section, make sure that **Solution** appears in the **Restore the following components** list. Then in the **Restore Only Configuration Settings** section, make sure that the **Restore content and configuration settings** option is selected. Next, in the **Restore Options** section, under **Type of Restore**, select the option that states **Same configuration**. Click on **OK** and then click on **Start Restore**.

Restore using PowerShell

To restore a service application by using Windows PowerShell, perform the following procedure:

1. Verify the user account requirements. Follow the procedure in the section titled **Farm Backup and Restore**, or visit TechNet at `http://technet.microsoft.com/en-us/library/ee748614.aspx`.

2. Open the SharePoint 2013 Management Shell (as an Administrator).

3. Type the following command (shown in cmdlet syntax) to perform the restore:

```
Restore-SPFarm -Directory <BackupFolder> -RestoreMethod Overwrite
-BackupId <GUID> -Item <SolutionPath>
```

A real world example will look as shown in the following command:

```
Restore-SPFarm -Directory \\DEV-SPS2013-A01\Backup -RestoreMethod
Overwrite -Item "farm\solutions"
```

Caveats and considerations

The following are caveats and considerations that should be understood:

• **Authored site elements**: These types of customizations include changes to master pages, cascading style sheets, forms, layout pages, content editor web parts, and so on. There is no formal backup or restore process for these items. Instead, they are backed up as part of the farm, web application, or content database with which they are associated.

- **Web.config files**: Changes to `Web.config` made via Central Administration or the SharePoint 2013 API and object model will be stored in the configuration database and can be recovered through farm or configuration backups. Changes made to `Web.config` outside of these methods will not be stored in the configuration database, and will need to be protected using file system backups. A special consideration is the `Web.config` file for forms-based authentication, which is manually edited and must be backed up using a file system backup.

- **Workflows**: Workflows can be backed up/restored, but there are many considerations. For example, declarative workflows are stored in content databases. Custom declarative workflows and workflows that depend on custom code have distributed components which must be accounted for. Additionally, workflows may interact with multiple site collections which means that those site collections need to be considered. For more information, visit `http://technet.microsoft.com/en-us/library/jj937239.aspx`.

- **Sandboxed solutions**: These solution packages are deployed to a single site collection and are stored in the associated content database. They cannot be backed up or restored individually, but will be included as part of a farm, web application, site collections, or content database backup or restore.

- **Customizations not packaged as solutions**: These types of customizations can be difficult to isolate, as customization resources may not be stored in standardized places, and SharePoint will not automatically back up anything outside of its defined scope. Be sure to consult with your developers and vendors to determine the make-up of your customization and component locations.

- **Third-party products**: Any third-party products deployed as solutions will be protected by SharePoint 2013 backup. Any third-party products not packaged as solutions fall under the same set of consideration as mentioned in the previous bullet point.

Site collection backup and restore

A site collection backup will include all of the sites and site resources belonging to the site collection. This option is intended for situations where you may need to restore a specific site collection only. Site collection backups can be performed through the Central Administration GUI, Windows PowerShell, and by using STSADM. However, restores can only be performed through Window PowerShell or STSADM.

Back up using the Central Administration GUI

To back up a site collection by using the Central Administration website, perform the following procedure:

1. Verify the user account requirements. Follow the procedure in the section titled **Farm Backup and Restore**, or visit TechNet at `http://technet.` `microsoft.com/en-us/library/ee748614.aspx`.

2. Open up the **Central Administration** home page, look in the **Backup and Restore** section, and click on **Perform a site collection backup**.

3. On the **Site collection backup** page, select the site collection from the **Site collection** list.

4. In the **Filename** box, type the local path of the backup file (for example, `\\DEV-SPS2013-A01\Backup\Backup.bak`), and then click on **Start Backup**.

Back up using PowerShell

To back up a site collection by using Windows PowerShell, perform the following procedure:

1. Verify the user account requirements. Follow the procedure in the section titled **Farm Backup and Restore**, or visit TechNet at `http://technet.` `microsoft.com/en-us/library/ee748614.aspx`.

2. Open the SharePoint 2013 Management Shell (as an Administrator).

3. Type the following command (shown in cmdlet syntax) to perform the backup:

```
Backup-SPSite -Identity <SiteCollectionGUIDorURL> -Path
<BackupFile> [-Force] [-NoSiteLock] [-UseSqlSnapshot] [-Verbose]
```

A real world example will look as shown in the following command:

```
Backup-SPSite -Identity http://dev-sps2013-a01 -Path \\DEV-
SPS2013-A01\Backup\Backup.bak
```

Restore using PowerShell

To restore a site collection by using Windows PowerShell, perform the following steps:

1. Verify the user account requirements. Follow the procedure in the section titled **Farm Backup and Restore**, or visit TechNet at `http://technet.` `microsoft.com/en-us/library/ee748614.aspx`.

2. Open the SharePoint 2013 Management Shell (as an Administrator).

3. Type the following command (shown in cmdlet syntax) to perform the restore:

```
Restore-SPSite -Identity <SiteCollectionURL> -Path <Backup
file> [-DatabaseServer <DatabaseServerName>] [-DatabaseName
<ContentDatabaseName>] [-HostHeader <Host header>] [-Force]
[-GradualDelete] [-Verbose]
```

A real world example will look as shown in the following code:

```
Restore-SPSite -Identity http://dev-sps2013-a01 -Path \\DEV-
SPS2013-A01\Backup\Backup.bak
```

Caveats and considerations

The following are caveats and considerations that should be understood:

- **Farm Performance**: Backing up a site collection will affect farm performance while the backup is running. Consider scheduling during off-peak times. If the site collection you are restoring is greater than 1 GB, you can use the Gradual Delete parameter for better performance. This will cause the data in the marked site collection to be deleted gradually, using a timer job, instead of all at once, which reduces the impact on server performance.

- **Other native backups**: Farm-level and content-database-level backup and restore can also be used for site collection recovery if a single site collection is stored in a database.

- **Lock Status**: If the site collection's Lock status is set to Not locked or Adding content prevented, SharePoint 2013 temporarily sets the site to read-only while the backup operation is occurring. SharePoint 2013 does this to reduce the possibility of users changing the site collection while it is being backed up. After the backup is complete, the setting is changed back its normal status.

- **Offline content**: If content is taken off-line for editing, once the content is restored, the server will automatically synchronize off-line content, which could result in data loss on the user's copies of the material.

Apps backup and restore

Apps for SharePoint are small, standalone applications intended to solve a specific business or end user need. Unlike features and solutions, apps for SharePoint can be installed by site owners to individual sites. SharePoint app components are stored in the content databases of the site collections where they are installed, in the farm configuration database, and in the Secure Store Service and App Management service applications.

All of these constructs need to be accounted for during backups and restores, and unfortunately, there is no singular procedure, although either Central Administration or Windows PowerShell can be used to perform all of the individual steps.

Backup

In order to properly back up an app, you have to follow these general steps:

1. Back up the content databases. Follow the procedure described earlier in this chapter, and visit the following link for additional information: `http://technet.microsoft.com/en-us/library/ee428327.aspx`.

2. Back up the farm configuration database. Follow the procedure described earlier in this chapter, and visit the following link for additional information: `http://technet.microsoft.com/en-us/library/ee428320.aspx`.

3. Back up the `Secure Store Service application` database. Visit the following link for additional information: `http://technet.microsoft.com/en-us/library/ee748648.aspx`.

4. Back up the `App Management application` database. Follow the procedure regarding service application backups described earlier in this chapter, and refer to the following link for additional information: `http://technet.microsoft.com/en-us/library/ee428318.aspx`.

5. Back up all of the site collections that host apps for SharePoint in your environment. Follow the procedure regarding site collection backups described earlier in this chapter.

Restore

In order to properly restore an app, you essentially have to perform the reverse the previous sequence of steps. Carry out the following general steps:

1. Restore the content databases. Follow the procedure regarding content database restores described earlier in this chapter, and visit the following link for additional information: `http://technet.microsoft.com/en-us/library/ee748604.aspx`.

2. Restore the farm configuration database. Follow the procedure regarding content database restores described earlier in this chapter, and visit the following link for additional information: `http://technet.microsoft.com/en-us/library/ee428326.aspx`.

3. Restore the `Secure Store Service application` database. Visit the following link for additional information: `http://technet.microsoft.com/en-us/library/ee748602.aspx`.

4. Restore the `App Management application` database. Follow the procedure regarding service application restores described earlier in this chapter, and visit the following link for additional information: `http://technet.microsoft.com/en-us/library/ee428305.aspx`.

5. Restore the site collections that host apps for SharePoint in your environment. Follow the procedure regarding site collection restores described earlier in this chapter.

Caveats and considerations

The following are caveats and considerations that should be understood:

- **Farm performance**: Backing up apps will affect farm performance due to all of the correlating events that have to occur. Consider scheduling backups on off-peak times.

- **Database versioning**: The content, configuration, and Secure Store Service and App Management service databases should all be backed up at the same time. Conversely, the same versions of each database should be restored at the same time for data consistency.

- **Remote components**: Any apps for SharePoint that contain remote components that are present in the backup copy of a site collection could cause issues, because two copies of the app could potentially be accessing the remote connection at the same time, which could lead to information disclosure or data loss.

- **Secure store service**: Backup of the Secure Store Service includes the use of a passphrase. Make sure that you record the passphrase during backup, as you will need to use this passphrase to restore the Secure Store database.

Sites, lists, and libraries – backup and restore

Sites, lists, and libraries can be exported via Central Administration or Windows PowerShell. This method is intended for restoring items, or moving/copying items from one farm or another. You can import a site, list, or document library from a backup of the current farm, a backup of another farm, or from a read-only content database. However, imports can only be performed through Window PowerShell.

Another method, although more restrictive, is to save your SharePoint site, list, or library as a template, by creating a Web Solution Package that will get stored in the Solution Gallery for the SharePoint site collection. Note that this method is not supported for sites using the Publishing feature.

Backup using the Central Administration GUI

To export a site, list, or library by using the Central Administration website, carry out the following procedure:

1. Verify the user account requirements. Follow the procedure in the section titled **Farm Backup and Restore**, or visit TechNet at `http://technet.microsoft.com/en-us/library/ee748614.aspx`.

2. Open up the **Central Administration** home page, and click on **Backup and Restore**, as shown in the following screenshot:

3. On the **Backup and Restore** page, in the **Granular Backup** section, click on **Export a site or list**, as depicted in the following screenshot:

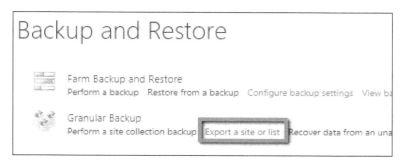

4. On the **Site Or List Export** page, in the **Site Collection** section, select the site collection from the **Site Collection** list, and then select the site from the **Site** list. If you are exporting the entire site, go to the next step. If you are exporting a list or library, select the list or library form the **List** list, as highlighted in the following screenshot:

5. In the **File location** section, in the **Filename** box, type the UNC path of the shared folder and the file to which you want to export the list or document library. The file name must use the `.cmp` extension, for example, `\\DEV-SPS2013-A01\Backup\Backup.cmp` (as shown in the previous screenshot).

6. If you want to export all of the security and permissions settings with the list or library, in the **Export Full Security** section, select the **Export full security** check box (as highlighted in the previous screenshot).

7. If you want to specify which version of the list or library to export, select one of the values (**All Versions**, **Last Version**, **Current Version**, **Last Major**, and **Last Minor**) in the **Export Versions** section from the **Export versions** list, and click on **Start Export**.

Backup using PowerShell

To export a site, list, or library by using Windows PowerShell, perform the following procedure:

1. Verify the user account requirements. Follow the procedure in the section titled **Farm Backup and Restore**, or visit TechNet `http://technet.microsoft.com/en-us/library/ee748614.aspx`.

2. Open the SharePoint 2013 Management Shell (as an Administrator).

3. Use the following cmdlet (shown in cmdlet syntax) to perform the backup:

```
Export-SPWeb -Identity <SiteURL> -Path <Path and File Name>
[-ItemUrl <URL of Site, List, or Library>] [-IncludeUserSecurity]
[-IncludeVersions] [-NoFileCompression] [-GradualDelete]
[-Verbose]
```

A real world example will look as shown in the following command:

```
Export-SPWeb -Identity http://dev-sps2013-a01 -Path \\DEV-SPS2013-A01\Backup\Backup.cmp -IncludeUserSecurity
```

Restore using PowerShell

To import a site, list, or library by using Windows PowerShell, perform the following procedure:

1. Verify the user account requirements. Follow the procedure in the section titled **Farm Backup and Restore**, or visit TechNet `http://technet.microsoft.com/en-us/library/ee748614.aspx`.

2. Open the SharePoint 2013 Management Shell (as an Administrator).

3. Use the following cmdlet (shown in cmdlet syntax) to perform the restore:

```
Import-SPWeb -Identity <SiteURL> -Path <ExportFileName> [-Force]
[-NoFileCompression] [-Verbose]
```

A real world example will look as shown in the following command:

```
Import-SPWeb -Identity http://dev-sps2013-a01 -Path \\DEV-
SPS2013-A01\Backup\Backup.cmp -Force
```

SharePoint templates

When you save your SharePoint site as a template, you are saving the overall framework of the site its lists and libraries, views and forms, and workflows. You can also include the contents of the site in the template such as the documents stored in the document libraries, and the list items stored in lists. You can also save lists and document libraries as templates to move data or documents from one site to another.

Caveats and considerations

The following are caveats and considerations that should be understood:

- **SharePoint version and edition constraints**: You cannot import a site, list or library exported from one version and restore to another (for example, from SharePoint 2010 Foundation to SharePoint 2013 Foundation), nor can you import/export between editions (for example, from SharePoint 2013 Foundation to SharePoint 2013 Server).

- **Item versioning**: When backing up and restoring sites, libraries, or lists, you will need to take item versioning into consideration. To specify which version of the site, list, or document library to include, use the `IncludeVersions` parameter (visit `http://technet.microsoft.com/en-us/library/ff607895.aspx` for details).

- **User permissions**: To include the user permissions associated with the list or document library, use the `IncludeUserSecurity` parameter (visit `http://technet.microsoft.com/en-us/library/ff607895.aspx` for details).

- **Compression**: In certain situations, it can be helpful to use the `NoFileCompression` parameter to prevent file compression during the export process, which will conserver resource usage . Using this parameter will result in a backup folder being created instead of a compressed file. Note that if you use this parameter in the export process, you will also need to use it in the import process.

- **Import granularity**: There is no option in the `Import-SPWeb` cmdlet to import a subset of the items within the export file. Everything in the specified export file will be imported.

- **Site template limitations**: The default site template is 50 MB. Also, many objects and features are not supported in a site template ,including list item version history, running workflow instances, taxonomy field values, and so on. Site templates are also not supported for sites using the "Publishing" feature. For more information, visit the following link: `http://msdn.microsoft.com/en-us/library/jj938033.aspx`.

Summary

This chapter covered the different SharePoint 2013 native backup and restore options with regard to all of the components that are part of a typical SharePoint 2013 farm. As mentioned before, SharePoint is a platform, and one that evolves and expands over time. The application/utilization of the platform and the amount of data will only grow, and your organization will need to come up with effective and efficient ways of handling disaster recovery. The following table summarizes backup and restore scopes along with the tools that can be used for each:

Operation	Scope	Central Administration	PowerShell Cmdlets	STSADM Tool	SQL Server
Backup	Farm	✓	✓	✓	☒
	Farm Configuration	✓	✓	✓	☒
	Web Application	✓	✓	✓	Database components only.
	Service Applications	✓	✓	✓	Database components only.
	Content Database	✓	✓	✓	✓
	Customizations	✓	✓	✓	☒
	Site Collections	✓	✓	✓	☒
	Sites, Lists & Libraries	✓	✓	✓	☒
Restore	Farm	✓	✓	✓	☒
	Farm Configuration	✓	✓	✓	☒
	Web Application	✓	✓	✓	Database components only.
	Service Applications	✓	✓	✓	Database components only.
	Content Database	✓	✓	✓	✓
	Customizations	✓	✓	✓	☒
	Site Collections	☒	✓	✓	☒
	Sites, Lists & Libraries	☒	✓	✓	☒

There are many best practices to consider, both technical and procedural, but the most important thing to understand about backup and recovery is where your limits are and what you actually can and cannot do. For additional help, the authors recommend you start by reviewing the following information:

- Backup and restore SharePoint 2013: `http://technet.microsoft.com/en-us/library/ee662536.aspx`.

- Backup and restore best practices in SharePoint 2013: `http://technet.microsoft.com/en-us/library/gg266384.aspx`.

However, backup and recovery tools are only one thing to consider.

The next chapter deals with enterprise data and dives into disaster recovery with respect to large data sets.

6
Working with Data Sizing and Data Structure

This chapter introduces the reader to SharePoint Disaster Recovery with different data sizing and data structures, and appropriate approaches to different SharePoint deployment scenarios and technical situations.

The reader may be wondering, what does data sizing and structure mean and how does it relate to SharePoint? It refers to the overall design selected that reflects the planned scale of a system. Within the context of a SharePoint farm, looking from the web applications, it is the selection of managed paths, site collections, hierarchy of sites and libraries, and distribution of site collections across content databases, as well as overall standards and system settings.

In most cases in organizations, SharePoint architecture and size limitations are viewed through the business requirements and performance keyhole rather than checking how quickly we can restore data, if there is a problem. This chapter views architecture from the second perspective, and will cover the following points:

- Understanding data sizing architectural choices within a SharePoint environment
- Working with very large amounts of data for recovery purposes
- Architecting a SharePoint topology with Disaster Recovery in mind

For the reader to be able to take action after reading this chapter, they must have read the previous chapters and understood the backup and restore methods of SharePoint.

 To implement a SharePoint DR approach with knowledge from this book, this chapter should be discussed in detail with the farm administrator and the SQL administrator, in order to discuss procedures. In fact, use this chapter as an agenda for the meeting.

Here's a real world example. An insurance company with world-class network, storage, and servers needed to do an urgent restore from backup to the DR environment in another location. The content database and the lone site collection was 170 GB. Given existing bandwidth, the data transfer operation took 20 hours to complete, before the database restore could be started. The business expectation of a same-day restore was not met.

Understanding data sizing architectural choices for DR

In SharePoint 2013 — like the previous versions — with very few exceptions, all content is stored in SQL Server. This database structure is not much different from normal .NET web applications or previous versions of SharePoint. This SharePoint content is stored in over 20 databases that are created during the SharePoint installation. All of the default databases have specific purposes, for example, farm configuration information is stored in a configuration database.

The content itself is stored in multiple content databases. This is where only part of the farm needs to be recovered, typically a content database. An example is a corrupted site, or permanently overwritten document, forcing a restore operation. Simply put, the smaller the database to be restored, the faster the recovery time.

A secondary point to consider with overly-large content databases is the disk space during the restore process, as the standby server may have been provisioned to be of a smaller capacity.

Even Central Administration content is stored in its own content database. Yes, the administration pages are content, as are the health analyzer rules. In fact all web applications must have at least one content database, and a good design will scale to include many more as storage demands. The number of databases is likely to change throughout the life of the SharePoint farm.

A SharePoint deployment should have a dedicated instance of SQL Server. Microsoft does not support end-user changes to the schema of SharePoint databases, such as adding database triggers, adding indexes, or modifying existing indexes within tables.

For information on database types and descriptions, visit the following site:

`http://technet.microsoft.com/en-us/library/cc678868.aspx#Sec1`

Throughout this, the reader will read many variations and combinations of how to architect SharePoint from a data recovery standpoint. Although this chapter is not about architecting the SharePoint environment for performance, the reader should be aware that these design decisions affect not just DR but performance as well.

Key SharePoint limits to consider with DR

When planning DR for an enterprise-class SharePoint farm with thousands of users and terabytes of data, it is essential to design within the limits of SharePoint. Microsoft publishes a long list of soft and hard boundaries and limits within SharePoint. These have not changed significantly between 2010 and 2013.

An example of a hard boundary limit is the 2GB limit on the file size. This limit is based on the operating system and SQL Server limits, and involves no trade-off options. However it is not advisable to allow for 2GB uploads without first considering the DR implications of possible content database growth. If large uploads are required, plan to start with smaller site collections, so that content database growth can stay within the stated DR RTOs.

 Control the content growth by defining a reasonable maximum upload size.

The maximum number of site collections per farm is 500,000 personal sites (which are site collections) plus 250,000 for all other site templates. In practice, this number is so large that there is effectively no limit to the number of site collections. The sites can all reside on one web application or can be distributed across multiple web applications. The maximum number of content databases per farm is 500. This is a soft limit. Exceeding this number only affects the administrative interface in Central Administration, and will not result in degradation in end-user perceived performance. When working on this scale, all administrative tasks should be performed using PowerShell, which handles long-running operations better than the Central Administrator browser interfaces.

From a recovery perspective, it is important to limit the size of content databases so that backup and restore is recoverable in an acceptable time frame. For example, if there are 50,000 site collections in a web application, how many content databases will that be, and how many of those collections will be in each database? This is key information to know for DR planning.

Content database size

Content database size has the most direct impact on any DR strategy. The limitations of hardware (bounded by the laws of physics) determine the speed of backups and restores.

 A prime example is restoring a single content database. The scenario is that a user one way or another destroys a document. It could be an upload over an existing document, replacing it completely using the explorer mode, or simply deleting a document and wanting it to be restored months later after the recycle bin has expired. The restore process is possible once there is an unattached database to extract the file, with the largest portion of the restore spent waiting for the restore to complete.

However, a large content database of 200 GB or more requires the better part of a day to restore; or worse, there may be insufficient spare disk space available for the restore. This size is within the recommendations by Microsoft for performance, but does have an impact on the time frames of DR.

Managing content database growth

The following table shows the settings that can be set to manage the growth of content databases in order to ensure DR recovery times are within acceptable time frames:

Level	Setting	Purpose
Web application	Maximum upload size	Limit the maximum size of files that can be uploaded.
Web application	Recycle bin	Duration to retain entries; can affect content database size.
Site collection	Quotas	Set a quota to ensure that content database sizes are manageable.
Library	Version settings	Can restrict the number of versions retained, in order to manage content database growth.

Allowing huge uploads, unlimited document versions, and no site quotas can each cause unconstrained growth, resulting in rapidly-growing content databases that can cause RTO to exceed committed time frames.

Tuning of the previous settings can be done via a script. The following example programmatically sets the maximum upload size to 100MB:

```
$webApplication = Get-SPWebApplication http://SharePoint
$webApplication.MaximumFileSize = 100 #in MB
$webApplication.WebApplication.Update()
```

Setting quotas via PowerShell is covered later in this chapter.

DR impact of design decisions

The impact of design decisions are of importance during a partial recovery, where only part of the farm needs to be recovered. An example is a corrupted site, or a permanently overwritten document forcing a restore operation. The design has a direct effect on the planned size of content databases. SharePoint farms that evolve through organic growth or by poor design practices can lead to the use of a single, huge site collection, which in turn results in huge content databases. Backing up and restoring huge content databases require excessive time, and the availability of large storage pools.

A common challenge in large farms is not having clear naming standards for all the parts that connect a URL back to a database. The greater the number of databases, the more crucial a clear mapping is for an administrator to be able to quickly and easily determine which database to restore during a recovery operation. If the administrator needs to spend an hour to trace a URL back to the database to restore, that's an extra unplanned hour in recovery timeframe.

 It is worse when an administrator recovers the wrong database.

These key decisions are summarized next, to explain how to control content databases of a manageable size that are logically mapped to their use:

- **Managed paths**: These are defined at the web application level, and provide the structure for additional site collections. A coherent managed path and site collection naming strategy is helpful for an administrator to be able to map a given URL or site collection back to a content database that might need to be restored. By default, sites is defined as a wildcard managed path. Better is to use Dept (for department), Div (for division), Company, or any other relevant way to break down content into logical content databases.

- **Host-named site collections**: Aside from search, this is the largest infrastructure change in SharePoint 2013. It's geared to allow for cloud-based multi-tenancy, and scalability beyond what can be done with the relatively-structured managed paths. Best is to select one web application, and use that for all host-named site collections.

- **Number of site collections**: Some users feel comfortable within the confines of a single site collection. There are certainly conveniences within a site collection, including shared security groups, shared content types, and an immediate, navigable hierarchy. Going with monolithic site collections limits any ability to scale across content databases, as a site collection can only ever exist within one content database. Once a site collection has grown too large, splitting it can be fraught with challenges. A large content database takes proportionately longer to backup, and more importantly, to recover. For DR purposes, the smaller the content databases, the faster the recovery time for a partial recovery scenario.

Going with a more hierarchical design with more site collections, will allow content database sizes to be more manageable, thereby speeding recover time with any one content database to recover during a partial recovery scenario.

A good approach when working with users is to play down the name (site collection, site, library, and folder) and focus instead on the hierarchy, which users understand. One can always tune navigation to give them an optimal experience. Steering the design to maximize the number of site collections will ultimately provide flexibility on content database sizing that will allow a faster RTO, thereby improving the DR plan.

> Once a content database becomes too large to restore within the DR RTO timeframe, it can be difficult to fix. Trying to reduce the size of content databases once populated with content is challenging if the underlying site collection is large and monolithic. The granularity of site collections is difficult to change later because it involves splitting content into new site collections, which inevitably changes the URLs. Moreover, copies of site collections cannot coexist within the same content database. Design thoughtfully up-front, and avoid pain later!

Establishing conventions

Disaster Recovery doesn't occur on a schedule. More likely disaster hits an inopportune time. It's 3 a.m., and a restore is needed; can an administrator easily determine which content database to restore? It's time for some conventions to make restore decisions a snap.

Database naming

The primary naming convention to put in place is the database naming standard, which enables an administrator to quickly identify the correct database for a restore. By default, SharePoint puts a **Globally Unique Identifier** (**GUID**) at the end of every database name. This is to ensure that two SharePoint farms can use the same database server without any conflict. However, the GUIDs make memorizing a database name practically impossible.

The Appendix to this book states basic naming conventions to consider adopting in best practices.

DR with a multiserver farm

SharePoint architecture starts with actual servers, followed by web applications, site collections, sites, lists, and the actual content itself, such as word documents and list items.

The more servers within a farm, the more involved the DR process is, in terms of documentation, planning, and deployment. Taking the other extreme, if everything is on a single server, web app, and site collection, the server may degrade under load and volume. SharePoint is designed for scaling across servers, both horizontally (redundant servers) and vertically (with dedicated server roles), so a growing number of servers in an enterprise farm is largely unavoidable.

In SharePoint 2013, the architecture demands more servers than in SharePoint 2010. (Of course, this is Microsoft). There is a greater need for extra servers for search, and there is a requirement to have a dedicated server for office web applications. As the number of servers increase, the management responsibility increases, requiring us to understand how these technologies work, and how to manage these servers to make them sing in unison.

Challenges with multiple servers

Multiserver issues include the following:

- Determining which server has logs related to a user issue. User traffic is balanced between web servers, and balanced between application servers. Tracing any one correlation ID can require checking more than one **Unified Logging Service** (**ULS**) log, or falling back on the SharePoint logging database, with its inevitable lags in log event acquisition.

- Ensuring file/storage/software/server configuration consistency across servers.

- Documenting and possibly automating the setting of which services are to run on each server.

Remember, one must know what service packs and hotfixes have been applied, if one doesn't want to be really surprised during the restore process when finding the restored content doesn't matches the patch level of the server. This can be found out from the control panel on each server. This should be noted in the technical documentation. Better, save every bit of software, **Cumulative Update (CU)**, and service pack applied to each server, both on the server and in a dedicated drive off the server.

A DR plan must consider all the contributing factors and how they work together.

SQL aliases

SharePoint architecture components that rely on SQL Server databases can all be redeployed to different SQL servers to balance server load and manage the risk of downtime, as parallel restores can be done. Best is to use aliases, making SQL Server redirection much easier than hard-coding actual SQL Server names. This is particularly important at SharePoint Server installation time, as the reference to the farm's Config database gets set at the time of installation.

This is done via the SQL Client Configuration Utility on the SharePoint server, which is the CLIConfig.exe application, and a matching alias defined on SQL Server using SQL Server Configuration Manager. This makes it easier to have a farm come up pointing to a different SQL Server for some databases, requiring only a change to the alias definition, and without a change in SharePoint.

Refer to setting up an alias on SQL Server at: http://msdn.microsoft.com/en-us/library/ms190445(v=sql.110).aspx.

When setting up the alias, there is the option, for a more secure approach, to use a custom port rather than the default SQL port. If this route is taken, be sure to configure a firewall rule to open the port on the inbound side of SQL Server. This is one example of what has to be a part of the DR plan. The DR plan depends upon the recovery SQL Server having both the aliases defined and the firewall rule configured.

Always use SQL aliases.

Content database size targets

The primary architectural decisions determine the size of content databases, which tend to be the largest databases in the SharePoint farm. When SharePoint 2010 was launched, the recommended soft limit was 100 GB. This was increased to 200 GB around the time of Service Pack 1. In SharePoint 2013, that recommendation has not been changed.

In order to leave sufficient room for growth, I always try to limit the initial content database size to 50GB, to allow room for organic growth. To enable that, the size of site collections has to be limited.

If a site collection is approaching 50 GB, or is expected to do so, it is best to use a dedicated content database. Site collection, which can be easily moved between content databases, is described later in this chapter.

It is highly recommended that if the site collection size is greater than 100 GB; store it in a dedicated content database; the reason being that this will help in backup and restore of the database when this is done from SQL Server or from SharePoint Central Administrator. Even better is to try to limit the content databases to 50 GB by having such site collections having their own content database.

For DR planning, the smaller the databases, the faster one can recover any one database. So DR planning is a bigger driver for managing database sizes, than SharePoint limitations.

 Note that one or more backup operations can place sufficient load on resources to impact end user perceived performance. Hence, backups should be scheduled during off-hours to the extent feasible.

Plan before going live

It is best to plan ahead and perform scenario analysis upfront, prior to ramping up all enterprise users onto a production SharePoint farm. This might seem obvious, but the urgency tends to crowd out the more important strategic long-term efforts.

Database management strategy changes the frequency of a backup; the RTO, RPO, and ROL must still be met. This was discussed in *Chapter 1, Planning and Key Concepts - What Not to Forget.*

Recovery Time Objective (RTO): How long it will take to recover from a disaster?

Recovery Point Objective (RPO): How much data can I afford to lose?

Recovery Level Objective (RLO): How granular must the recovery capability be?

Major oversights

One area of oversight is to understand and manage the relationships between content in a content database, and dependencies outside the content database. Examples include references to features and service applications.

Content dependencies

A given page in a SharePoint content database could have the following things:

- A master page referencing files in the 15 Hive.

- Any web application, site collection, or web feature that is enabled in the content database but not deployed as a farm solution on the DR farm.

- A search web part dependent on enterprise search.

- An Excel web part dependent on Excel services configuration, including references to an Excel spreadsheet, and a dependency on the spreadsheet location being registered as a trusted location.

- A PerformancePoint web part dependent on the PerformancePoint service application configured.

- Taxonomy fields used in libraries for document tagging that are dependent on a managed metadata service application being configured.

- An external list that is dependent on an external content type registered and permissioned within **Business Connectivity Services (BCS)**, as well as a dependency on an application ID defined in the Secure Store Service application.

These are just a few gotchas that should be known prior to the users simmering during an unscheduled downtime or delayed recovery.

BCS is an integration component of SharePoint that allows power users and developers to interact with external data from enterprise applications, web services, and data services. For more information on BCS in SharePoint 2013, visit `http://msdn.microsoft.com/en-us/ library/jj163782.aspx`. Managed metadata services enable the use of taxonomies for tagging content. An overview of managed metadata service applications in SharePoint Server 2013 can be found at `http://technet. microsoft.com/en-us/library/ee424403.aspx`.

Managing content dependencies

The previous content dependency examples highlight how a content database restore can still result in broken functionality. When doing a content database restore to the same production server these issues should not occur, but when restoring to a different farm then the linkages between content and external dependencies needs to be understood and planned for.

Documenting content linkage

Understanding the linkages requires documentation of every use and reference to anything external to the site collection. As with all DR-related documentation, this must be stored or replicated off SharePoint. As ironic as that sounds, any documentation that is needed for DR needs to be accessible off the system around which DR is planned.

At a minimum, we need to document the site collection, the relevant URLs, the external reference, and a responsible point of contact. This information will guide both what to test for DR testing and real recovery operations, as well as for guiding the actual recovery steps for the planned scenarios.

Going one step further, the following information should be collected, based on the category:

Category	Documentation
Feature	Basic feature information including the following points: • Source code location • Source code version • Executable location • FeatureID (GUID) • Purpose • Feature Scope (farm, web app, site, web) • Web configuration changes (if any)
Local server reference	References to any server files should be kept to a minimum, but documented when used.
Excel services	Functional use of Excel services may require the following configuration settings: • Trusted data connection library locations • Trusted file locations • UDF assemblies, if used
Managed metadata services	For taxonomy use, this is simply the term set group and term set used.
PerformancePoint services	Like Excel services, the PerformancePoint service application needs to be aware of what locations to trust, including the following ones: • Data source locations • Content locations
Search	Local search functionality can be dependent on the following centrally managed settings: • Scopes • Managed properties
Business data connectivity services	Any local external list or use of an ECT (External Content Type) is dependent on the following things: • A named ECT, configured with specific user access • A mapping to a Secure Store application ID, unless Kerberos is configured and used for identity management • The availability of the data source that the ECT is mapped to, which is frequently a SQL Server source, but can be another source with a dependency on a .NET assembly

Category	Documentation
Secure Store services	Commonly-used services with ECT are as follows: • Named application ID • Credentials mapped for access • Specific permissions that need to be granted
Access services and Visio services	These are simpler configurations, but any dependency should be documented as well.

Collecting this documentation can be a challenge, as it is historical in nature, requiring a bit of systems archaeology.

Content dependency governance

The challenge with all such documentation is maintaining it while going forward. This is best achieved through a governance process. While SharePoint governance is a topic in its own right, this can be achieved via a release process. Every feature, deployment, or enhancement in production should go through a change control process. This is the point where a planned change is documented in the DR plan, along with the previous information to enable recovery. Every proposed deployment should be accompanied by a form (in writing or online) that probes for its use in relation to SharePoint. Any proposed use of an external dependency in SharePoint must be documented for inclusion in the DR plan, and slated to be included in periodic DR testing.

Know the external content dependencies; plan and include them in the recovery testing. Proactive SharePoint leaders establish governance to keep the DR plan up-to-date.

RBS

RBS (Remote Blob Storage) is a technique for dramatically reducing the size of content databases by using external filestream storage for databases larger than a given size. This is basically a set of file directories that are system managed. From a DR perspective, it offers no benefit. However, one needs to know if any part of a farm is using RBS. When using RBS, it is imperative that the backups include a time-synchronized copy of the mapped filestream. Without the filestream backup/restore, the content database could respond normally until a file from the filestream is referenced.

By design, RBS employs lazy deletes. The reason this is done is in case a restore operation is not perfectly synchronized with the filestream restore operation. There is a user-configurable delay between a requested document delete, and when it is actually deleted from the filestream. Lowering the delay allows faster recovery of disk utilization, but slightly increases the risk of a deletion-synchronization issue.

 Know whether RBS is enabled on a farm and include it in the DR planning.

BlobCache

BlobCache is a great technique for caching content on the server, or even on the client, for faster end-user perceived performance and lower database load. However, in a restore scenario, it is easy for the BlobCache to get out of sync with the content databases. The best approach to avoid such issues is to add a step into any recovery operation to clear out the BlobCache.

The following PowerShell script is per web application:

```
$webApp = Get-SPWebApplication "http://
sharepoint"[Microsoft.SharePoint.Publishing.PublishingCac
he]::FlushBlobCache($webApp)
```

It is good to know that BlobCache is enabled on a web application, and plan to flush it on any content or server restore operation.

SharePoint_Config

One of the most common restore scenarios is restoring the farm configuration database. There is exactly one `SharePoint_Config` database per farm. This is normally a very small but absolutely crucial database. Note that the farm configuration database will never need to be restored to a DR site. Each farm has its own configuration database. When restoring this database, the farm is generally totally offline, and the time to recover is absolutely crucial. The smaller this database can be made, the faster it can be recovered during a disaster.

Here's a real world example. An e-commerce company backup started failing due to uncontrolled growth of the `SharePoint_Config` database. This was traced to the timer job history and was subsequently reconfigured and fixed.

Under some scenarios, this database can grow dramatically. This is because the timer job history is stored there, and is cleaned out weekly by yet another timer job. The current duration for retaining this history can be set with the following PowerShell commands:

```
$TJ = Get-SPTimerJob | Where-Object {$_.name -eq "job-delete-job-history"}
```

```
$TJ.daystokeephistory
```

The following command is used to determine when the job last ran:

```
$TJ.get_LastRunTime()
```

To reduce the number of days of history to retain, in order to keep the `config` database to a manageable size, use the following commands:

```
$TJ.set_DaysToKeepHistory(3)
```

```
$TJ.update()
```

 The authors suggest changing the clean-up frequency to run daily, to reduce the periodic growth.

This can be done in Central Administrator, under monitoring, review job definitions. That way the backup will run faster, and any possible restore operation will also be commensurately quicker.

Getting a handle on a farm

In order to design a DR plan, one needs to understand data sizing of the farm. Here are the steps one can take to gather the information needed to understand the existing farm and estimate its growth. This will provide a clear understanding of the size of the backups, so planning for recovery time frames is possible, and will also provide insights into the rate of growth and on quotas that can govern the growth of databases.

Here's a real world example. It happens every day. An administrator is hired to manage and maintain a SharePoint farm and put DR in place. There's no documentation. This should be avoided.

One can't manage what one can't measure.

Size of all SharePoint databases

To plan for DR, one needs to know the size of all databases to be backed up and restored. The following small script will produce a CSV report of the bytes per database attached to the SharePoint farm:

```
Get-SPDatabase | select name,DiskSizeRequired | convertto-csv | set-
content "C:\DBsize.csv"
```

RBS report

There is no direct mechanism in Central Administrator to view the RBS configuration. This script will give a report of the RBS settings throughout the farm. With the output of this script, one can determine if RBS is used within the farm, and if so, take this into account in the backup/restore plan, in order to ensure functionality on restore:

Here's a real world example. An administrator inherits a SharePoint farm. There's no indication anywhere in Central Administrator that this feature is enabled. He/she has no idea that the farm had RBS until he/she restored a content database. It restores fine, but the documents cannot be downloaded.

```
Get-SPContentDatabase | foreach {$_;
  try {
    $rbs = $_.RemoteBlobStorageSettings;
    write-host "Provider Name=$($rbs.GetProviderNames())";
    write-host "Enabled=$($rbs.enabled)";
    write-host "Min Blob Size=$($rbs.MinimumBlobStorageSize)"
  }
  catch {
    write-host -foregroundcolor red
      "RBS not installed on this database!`n"
  }
  finally {
    write-host "End`n"
  }
}
```

Site collection size report

It is useful to know the sizes of site collections, and their distribution among the content databases. Given that smaller content databases means faster restore operations, this is critical information for managing the size of content databases, and how they are allocated. A report can be generated on the size of each site collection within each content database within a given web application with the next given script. The output is a **CSV (Comma Separated Value)** file easily read into Excel. If there are a lot of site collections, just convert the report to a pivot table to see the distribution and sizes of site collections across the content databases.

```
get-spwebapplication http://SharePoint | Get-SPSite -Limit all |
select url,contentdatabase,@{label="Size in GB";Expression={$_.usage.
storage/1GB}} | convertto-csv | set-content "C:\TEMP\DBsize.csv"
```

Site collection sizes help you to choose how to rebalance content databases for optimal sizing in order to allow meeting an RTO.

One common situation is for MySites to be distributed unevenly across content databases, leading to some content databases being much larger than others. As discussed earlier, managing content database sizes is a key to meeting the RTO.

Quota report

Setting quotas puts limits on site collection growth. It also provides the administrator with a weekly notification of the site collections that have exceeded a preset warning size.

The following report generates a list of all the quotas in place across a web application:

```
$webapp = Get-SPwebapplication "http://SharePoint"
$webapp | get-spsite -Limit ALL | ForEach-Object {
  $site = $_;
  $site;
  $site.quota;
}
$site.dispose()
$webapp.dispose()
```

Look for site collections that have no quotas. These represent opportunities for unconstrained growth without notification, which could result in content database growth that exceeds the RTO targets.

This report can be scheduled by creating a Task Manager scheduled report to run weekly. Configure it to run even when the user is not logged on; configure an authorized service account to run the report. Best is to put scripts that are scheduled to run regularly into a dedicated server folder named as PRODUCTION_TASKS. Have the Task Manager trigger a .BAT file that calls the previous quota script and extend it to trigger an e-mail with the results. The .BAT file would refer to the following PowerShell script:

```
POWERSHELL -command "& 'C:\\PRODUCTION_TASKS\QuotaReport.ps1'"
```

Managing growth

A solid DR plan can evolve into disarray if content database growth is unconstrained. As a content database size increases, the speed to recover slows proportionately. In the previous sections we established the metrics for working within SharePoint limits, and reporting on sizing. Once there is a complete picture of the SharePoint farm, one can take steps to manage its growth.

 Recommendation: Monitor database growth on a weekly basis. Any large growth merits a conversation with business users to understand the change in behavior. Often the growth is tied to a new use for SharePoint that can possibly be addressed with a separate dedicated content database to maintain manageable database sizes for rapid DR recovery.

Setting quotas

To set a quota on a site collection, carry out the following steps:

1. From Central Administration, in the application management section, click on **Configure quotas and locks**.

 Site Collections
Create site collections   Delete a site collection   Confirm site use and deletion
Specify quota templates   Configure quotas and locks   Change site collection administrators
View all site collections   Configure self-service site creation

2. Set the Site lock information to Adding content prevented.

3. Set the **Site Quota Information** to meet requirements as follows, and then click on OK:

Here's a scripted approach for how to set quotas across all site collections in a web application:

```
$webApplication = Get-SPWebApplication http://SharePoint
$TemplateName = "Preferred Quota Template"
$contentService = [Microsoft.SharePoint.
   Administration.SPWebService]::ContentService
$quotaTemplate = $contentService.QuotaTemplates[$TemplateName]

if ($quotaTemplate -ne $null)
{
  $webApplication.Sites | ForEach-Object {
  if ($_.url -match "http://SharePoint/MyPath*")
  {
    $_.url
    try {
      $_.Quota = $quotaTemplate; } finally { $_.Dispose();}
    }
  }
}
```

Set quotas for every site collection, and take action on early size warning notifications.

Before running this script, define the quotas in Central Administration, to match the desired warning and storage limits.

Rebalancing content databases

Earlier in the chapter we established that managing content database size is critical to being able to perform a partial recovery within the target recovery time, where a single content database is restored. If one content database is not only larger than the target to meet the RTO, but also has more than one site collection, this is easily solved.

Site collections can be easily moved to another content database. The key restriction is that the target content database must already be attached to the same web application. Moving a site collection to a new content database should be done by using the `Move-SPSite` cmdlet.

See TechNet for details on the `Move-SPSite` cmdlet at `http://technet.microsoft.com/en-us/library/ff607915.aspx`.

If there isn't a spare small content database, simply first create a new content database attached to the target content database by using the `New-SPContentDatabase` cmdlet. Note that the target web application needs to be specified.

Actively manage content database sizes, to ensure the ability to rapidly restore any given content database.

See TechNote for details on the `New-SPContentDatabase` cmdlet at `http://technet.microsoft.com/en-us/library/ff607572.aspx`

Restricting version retention

There are situations where documents are frequently edited. Each edit creates a new version in SharePoint. In SP2010, each version consumed the full disk space, with no optimization for managing deltas. In SP2013, one of the benefits of shredded storage is that it optimizes storage usage for multiple similar versions of not just Office XML (Office 2010/2013) documents but also other file types such as PDFs and image files. It does this by working out and storing only the file differentials. Even with shredded storage, the number of versions retained can be limited on document edits.

If users will accept it, it is best to put a finite limit on the number of document versions retained, to manage content growth.

Let's limit major versions to three, and minor versions to five. The following code shows how to do this across the farm:

```
$spWebApp = Get-SPWebApplication http://SharePoint
for ($Si=0; $Si -lt $spWebApp.Sites.count; $Si++)
{
  $site = $spWebApp.Sites[$Si];

  for ($Wi=0; $Wi -lt $site.AllWebs.count; $Wi++)
  {
    $web = $site.AllWebs[$Wi];

    for ($Li=0; $Li -lt $web.Lists.count; $Li++)
    {
      $List = $web.Lists[$Li];
      if ($list.EnableVersioning)
      {
        $list.MajorVersionLimit = 3
      }

      if ($list.EnableMinorVersions)
      {
        $list.MajorWithMinorVersionsLimit = 5
      }
      $list.Update()
    }
  $web.dispose()
  }
  $site.dispose()
}
$spWebApp.dispose()
```

Backup and restore plan

As stated in *Chapter 1, Planning and Key Concepts – What Not to Forget* and *Chapter 2, Creating, Testing, and Maintaining the DR Plan*, a backup and restore strategy is as follows:

- Develop recovery objectives
- Decide what to protect and restore

When the previous two bullets are defined, be sure to decide what can and cannot be lost in the SharePoint environment, and if any time delays can occur. Beyond that, content can be prioritized, both in terms of frequency of backup and the sequence of restoration.

Finally, construct the backup plan documentation. It is important to remember that they are dynamic. This means that they will change, because business requirements are changing; so meetings and regular reviews are necessary. Better is to keep the backup plan up-to-date by making it a part of the release cycle. Any changes flowing into production should document how the backup plan needs to be updated in order to accommodate the change.

 SharePoint backup plans must address data loss that might be caused by natural disasters, power outages, employee errors, hardware failures, and even lack of system upgrades.

The following scenario table can help to determine the backup and restore plan for the SharePoint environment:

Tool	Type of restorable objects	Maximum backup size supported	Supported backup type
SharePoint Farm Backup and Restore	• Farm • Search • Service • Web application • Content database • Site collection • Site • List item/document • Configurations • Customizations (if packaged as user solutions)	< 200 GB	Full Incremental
SQL Server	• Content database • Site (only if a single site collection is stored in a database) • List item/document	Content databases > 200 GB (may require additional management)	Full Differential
Windows PowerShell Site Collection Backup and Restore	• Site collection (not recommended for site collections larger than 80 - 100 GB)	100 GB	Full Differential
Windows PowerShell Import and Export	• Site (List or Doc Library) • List items • Customizations (if packaged as user solutions)	100 GB	Full

The following table shows common backup and restore scenarios and help define appropriate backup and restore plans:

Tool	Type of Restorable object
SharePoint farm backup and restore Central Administrator or PowerShell	• Farm • Search • Web application • Content database • Site collection • Site (web)
SQL Server	Content database
PowerShell	• Site collection • Site (web) • Library

The tool chosen for the backup and restore process depends on what is needed to protect in the SharePoint environment.

> Central Administration backup and restore is discussed in *Chapter 5, Central Administration and Other Native Backup and Restore Options*.

Answer the following questions, and then use the information provided in the previous table as a guide to help choose the correct backup and restore tools to meet the business requirements given the data sizing in your environment:

• How much time does the tool take to backup and restore content, and can processes be automated?

• How complete does the restore need to be for business functionality to return to normal?

• What backup type does this tool support (full, differential, or incremental)?

• How difficult is this tool to manage? Are new skills required? Is cross training of staff required?

Note that the tool has to work within the existing production and the DR framework. It can only back up and restore as fast as hardware will permit. This includes network, bandwidth to the DR site and storage speed. Compression and other techniques can help but are generally incremental. Benchmarking backup and recovery is a key to understanding the rate that an operation will proceed.

As stated in *Chapter 5, Central Administration and Other Native Backup and Restore Options*, the SharePoint server's restore processes can restore a farm from a farm backup that was created by using the SharePoint tools. Additionally, restore a farm, or portions of it, by restoring from a component backup that used a farm backup system. One can also use the unattached database feature for a content database by using either a backup or an export to connect to, in order to restore or import the data.

This is ideal for large-scale restore activities such as multiple web applications and hundreds of site collections.

There are a few points to remember while reviewing Microsoft SQL Server 2012 which will be helpful to understand performance and the disaster recovery process.

The authors recommend installing a dedicated instance of SQL Server on a separate server, but if it is required to install the SQL instance on a shared server, then configure the default memory setting, and specify dedicated memory for the SharePoint SQL server instance. Otherwise, the other application(s) running on that server might consume more memory and which will impact the overall performance of SharePoint 2013. Have a look at the following screenshot:

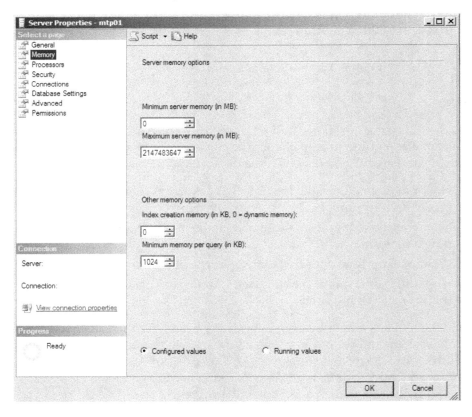

Configure the **Database default locations** to be on a different drive—either on the file system or on a different network-mapped path. If all the data files (`.mdf`), log files (`.ldf`), and backup files (`.bak`) are stored on the same drive and disaster happens, both the database server and underlying database files need to be restored together, leaving no recovery flexibility.

When this setting is changed, perform a SQL Server instance restart.

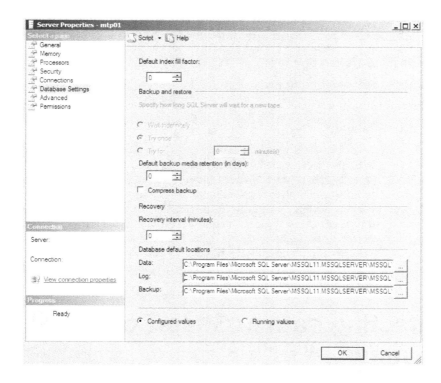

The authors recommend the full recovery model, with differential backup of the database. With this model, SQL Server preserves the transaction log until it is backed up. This allows you to use a DR plan that includes a combination of full and differential database backups, in conjunction with transaction log backups.

In order to configure a full recovery model, modify the model system database setting; whenever the new database created either directly from SQL Server or from SharePoint, it takes the default setting configured in the model system database.

Be aware with this setting transaction log growth needs to be carefully monitored and managed.

Tiering the recovery plan

Overnight daily tape backups of everything are a thing of the past. While tape can be part of the overall backup strategy, more systems today require almost no downtime, and can have **Recovery Point Objectives (RPO)** and **Recovery Time Objectives (RTO)** measured in minutes, not days. By selecting appropriate RPO and RTO, organizations can prioritize their business critical systems and tier recovery capabilities to match their business requirements.

One approach to RPO is to separate and prioritize data among disks. The following ranking should be used for prioritizing data among faster disks:

* TempDB and transaction logs
* Database transaction log files
* Search database
* Database data files

 What is the TempDB? It is the most important SharePoint SQL database. Many SharePoint performance issues are due to improper SQL configuration and more importantly, not giving enough thought to the TempDB itself. (Management of the TempDB, is a topic in itself.) Every action that SharePoint performs is staged in the TempDB before it is committed. When configuring TempDB in SQL Server, take care as it has a significant effect on SharePoint operations.

Architecting data in SharePoint with DR in mind

A good cliché is that DR is achieved by 3P's: Planning, Performing, and Practice; of a strategy that meets predefined organizational goals and objectives for business continuity.

Because every organization is unique with the demands of the business, do not use a *one size fits all* approach for a solution. Each environment needs to be approached from the perspective of identifying an appropriate approach.

- Design for high availability and disaster recovery first, then for performance and capacity.

- Understand the costs associated with a DR plan, not just servers but manpower too. Remember that farm administrators are busy; they generally do not have spare time to be proactive and think about what should be done, unless senior IT management allocates time for them to do these activities.

- Design from the bottom to up: server capacity, network devices, installation, content databases, and then site collections.

Recovery and restore

Recovery is the short term process of getting things back up and running. It's like replacing a burst tire with a spare one; it is not a permanent solution, and one can't drive as far or as fast, but it gets one moving again quickly. What's the appropriate recovery strategy? How quickly can a company get back to business? And is that quick enough? All of these factors are important considerations that need to be addressed in any thorough business continuity backup plan.

The restore phase is about putting things back the way they were. As with the car example, one should not continue to drive on a spare tire, and the environment should not continue handling production loads from the recovery environment indefinitely. Businesses must ask themselves: does this current solution let us do that? Some popular virtualized backup solutions allow for a backup to a virtual machine, but don't allow a restore out of them. As a result, one has to ensure that processes are in place to restore a proper working environment, allowing a business to return to full functionality.

If a company goes live with a DR server, and users change content, can that content be brought back to the production server when ready to *fail back*? During hurricane Sandy, a financial firm did not use their fail-over process because of lack of confidence on the restore process.

 Have a well thought-out plan to support changes on your recovery server, so that the *fail back* to production can be done without losing those changes.

Further reading

The following are some links which provides you more information:

- *Microsoft virtual academy SQL Server for SharePoint 2013*: `http://www.microsoftvirtualacademy.com/`.

- *SharePoint 2010 versus SharePoint 2013 boundaries and limits comparison*: `http://www.khamis.net/blog/Lists/Posts/Post.aspx?ID=91`.

- *Software boundaries and limits for SharePoint 2013*: `http://technet.microsoft.com/en-us/library/cc262787.aspx`.

- *Overview of backup and recovery in SharePoint 2013*: `http://technet.microsoft.com/en-us/library/ee663490.aspx`.

- *Data protection and recovery*: `http://msdn.microsoft.com/en-us/library/ee536542.aspx`.

Summary

This chapter has outlined approaches and considerations for planning and accommodating the SharePoint data sizing, right-sized for an organization.

Plans are nothing; planning is everything...

The very definition of "emergency" is that it is unexpected, therefore it is not going to happen the way you are planning.

– Dwight D. Eisenhower

(From a speech to the National Defense Executive Reserve Conference in Washington, D.C. November 14, 1957)

The following chapter explains DR when the SharePoint has custom development within its environment.

7
Disaster Recovery with Custom Development

Each chapter of this book provides great insights, and useful practices, that will help you in creating a high fidelity **SharePoint** operation. In this chapter, we will look beyond the traditional admin role, and into the realm of the developer. The chapter's goal is to aid the developer in making things just a little bit easier for themselves and the administrator, particularly when a crisis occurs that requires our **Disaster Recovery (DR)** procedures to kick in.

This chapter explains how to implement a solid DR strategy for SharePoint custom development environments, and will cover the following topics:

- Getting familiar with SharePoint development
- Understanding the challenges
- Steps for providing a recovery plan for customizations

The basics

It is easy to overlook the complexities of operating a SharePoint environment from the lens of the developer, especially in cases where solid governance, change management, and configuration management does not exist as part of your regular IT service management procedures. Worse yet, it is quite common for a developer to take on administrative roles, thereby making assumptions and taking shortcuts, often from the perspective of "well I know what to do" or "I wrote the code, so I know what's going on".

This approach leads to late nights, and extended periods of downtime. Everyone knows that this is not the proper deployment approach to take, but it is often followed. The management must enforce a written release policy unless they want an uncomfortable status meeting with the business owners of SharePoint applications.

The fact is that each solution or customization has some effect on the overall fidelity of the platform. It is important to understand the following classic conventions:

- What is being deployed: code or business impact
- Where is it being deployed: GAG, Hive, bin or content database
- How is it being deployed: good to know if the functionality needs to be turned off or retracted

Remember, there can be multiple services involved, feature dependencies, and a ton of custom functionality behind what is visible to the user and even the administrator.

To cement this level of paranoia, I would like to share a story, which an electrician once shared with me. Big Billy told me about "the courtesy wrap".

He said, "A caring electrician will put a wrap of electrical tape around the contacts of every outlet or switch, which they install. The reason is simple. If the next guy is less caring or inexperienced, he might just reach in, and grab the outlet without turning off the power, thereby resulting in a jolt, damage, or potentially resulting in a serious electrocution. A few seconds and a little tape might go a long way to make someone's day a little brighter"(pun intended!).

Similarly, when it comes to SharePoint development, a little forward thinking can go a long way, too.

All developers understand the importance of designing supportability into their code. In practice it can be extremely difficult in a SharePoint environment because there are a lot of moving parts and deployment approaches. From the previous paragraphs, you may think there is a dissertation on development best practices. This is not going to happen in this chapter, because the best practices are very generic, and understanding the basics and communicating among your technical team is more important.

What is explained in this chapter is an overview of development practices that are necessary for a mission-critical SharePoint environment. How this helps disaster recovery is by maintaining a carefully tuned development lifecycle to ensure that custom code is most easily redeployed in a variety of restoration cases. In fact, as a developer the most important thing that we can do to facilitate restoration happens way before ever considering a restore.

Before we go into more detail, we have to start with a basic understanding of SharePoint Development, its implication on the restoration process, and how is it changing in SharePoint 2013.

The 3 Cs of SharePoint Development

The classic definition of software development is most often associated with programming or writing code, but to leverage the vast power of SharePoint, we must start to think of it as Solution Development, which could include: configuration, customization, and coding. In fact, it is not appropriate to use the word "could" when in nearly every solution it "will" involve all three C's – **Configure**, **Customize** and **Code**. These are defined in the following figure:

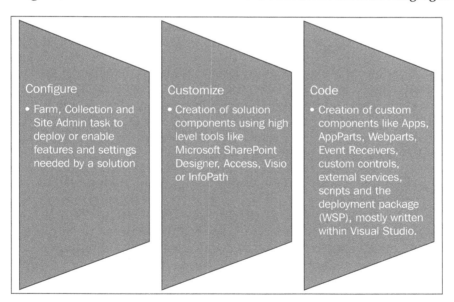

The first C of development, configuration, happens all over SharePoint, at the list, library, or site level using their respective settings, or at the site collection or farm level. By configuring SharePoint features, we enable or tune the functionality to best suit our desired purpose. For example, a contract management solution would undoubtedly require version control, workflows, check in/check out, and content approval.

These settings can be standardized, and are discussed later in the chapter, but for now, it is important to understand that the feature settings made at the site or site collection level will be stored within the content database along with the site. This will always be true, regardless of how this setting was implemented; manually using the browser, using SharePoint designer, using a PowerShell script, or through the object model and some custom code.

Feature settings at the farm level (made through **Central Administration**) most often affect a **Service Database**, but could also affect the SharePoint configuration database log file. In this case, this will always be true regardless of whether the change was made manually or though some automated method.

Note that, even if each service is a bit different in this regard, no service setting will be saved to the file system or to a content database.

Also, remember that some services create a slew of new timer jobs per web application. Thus, a simple little change can have a considerable performance impact even before our new solution gets deployed.

The second C of development, customization, can range from ultra-simple to fairly complex; from simply modifying some CSS to creating a theme using PowerPoint, a **Custom Master Page**, **SharePoint Designer Workflow**, a form using **InfoPath**, a dashboard using Excel and **Excel Services**, all the way to a fully baked application using Microsoft Access and SharePoint's **Access Services**. In fact, a well-designed business application will probably use a few of these.

Let's take an example of the common **Employee Time-off Request (ETR)**. An ETR will always include a form and workflow, and if you are keen on improving the business performance, a dashboard tracks the relevant KPIs: InfoPath, SharePoint designer workflows, and an Excel services dashboard. Of course, to start using these services we might have some prerequisite features to enable and settings to configure, as they are the necessary configuration level tasks for this solution.

For the most part, customization using the tools mentioned is stored within the content database for the site. However, the source artifacts (for example, the Access MDB, the InfoPath form, and the original artwork) needs to be maintained somewhere. That somewhere could be a file system, a source control system, or even SharePoint, but we certainly do not want to lose these artifacts in the event that we need to change something or restore something. As with all development, we sometimes need to go back to our source files.

It is also worth mentioning that it is common — actually necessary — for certain artifacts to be deployed to the Hive (`c:\Program Files\Microsoft\Common Files\...`), for example page layouts or images. In this case, we need to account for those files on the SharePoint server file system, and make sure that they remain in sync with the rest of the solution. Of course you should never deploy anything directly to the Hive; always use a solution (WSP) when deploying.

 The complexity mounts particularly at the end of a project.

When it comes to the final C, code, or the programmed parts of the solution, this is generally understood by most organizations which already have an experience in software development. For SharePoint, it is the thing those guys do using Visual Studio, but SharePoint has a way of making things just a little more interesting. While we can't devote time in this book to develop best practices in general, there are a few noteworthy considerations that will simplify future restoration, which is discussed later in this chapter.

1. When a farm solution is deployed properly (that is through a WSP solution file) the code portions (the code assemblies) get deployed to the **Global Assembly Cache (GAC)** or `C:\Windows\assembly`. Taking a quick look at the GAC you will immediately see that this is no ordinary folder, and each assembly has a version ID, allowing multiple versions of the same assembly within the GAC. Later we'll discuss how assembly versions place a critical role in recovery scenarios.

2. During the deployment, non-coded resources (for example, image files) are typically deployed to the Hive, making them available to all web applications on the farm.

The important point to remember is that the developer can pretty much do anything they want by writing a bit of code. That's the beauty of software. You can make it do pretty much anything. Of course, not understanding the details of what a particular solution does during deployment or its impact, and where it drops the resources will make for a very long and painful day when the time to recover from a disaster arrives.

With a basic definition of SharePoint development, we can explore some procedural areas that contribute to a high fidelity SharePoint operating environment. As you will see, achieving a high fidelity environment will simplify recovery procedures and reduce risk.

Accounting for things

Do you remember way back in kindergarten, when we each had an assigned cubby or basket to put our belongings in? Our teachers were smart. They didn't want to go looking for stuff when it was time to get ready to go home. Imagine the pandemonium of a bunch of kids running around the classroom, the teacher chasing them down, the bus driver honking the last call horn, and I still can't find my coat!

 The last thing we want to do during a crisis is look like a bunch of out of control children.

To the developer/SharePoint newbie, it might seem like SharePoint is out to get you. For sure it is not clearly evident where anything is. There is no manifest showing all the dependencies, or the bits that were changed or introduced since SharePoint was initially installed and configured. Sure, there are some lovely screens showing solutions deployed to the farm or to a sandbox, and you really want some detail from PowerShell, but there is no reporting information on what the solution impacts.

 As SharePoint administrators, we are blind to what each solution affected or what it may be doing behind the covers.

Some may say this is a governance issue. Others may say it is just common sense. To all of them I say, "So why aren't you doing anything about it?"

This can sound important by calling it **SharePoint Solution Governance (SPSG)**, where the technical teams align **Configuration Management** and **Change Management** procedures (that should make all the ITILers really think they are smart).

The SPSG works like this. Once developed, a solution requires a simple document before it can even be considered for integration test or deployment. The solution and its artifacts have to be placed in a well-defined location that will be there in the event of a crisis.

 Using your desktop is a really bad idea.

Finally, the solution will be deployed to test and staging farms (at least a couple of times) before it makes it to the production farm.

Of course, an SPSG document will be submitted along with our change request, and it will be placed in a reachable area for future reference. The SPSG document will define the "what and where" of our solution, and will state the following points:

- Solution name: This represents the name of the solution.
- Description: This describes what the solution does.
- Target servers: These are the servers where the solution is deployed to.
- Solution artifacts: This lists each part of the solution, for example, the WSP name, administrator instructions, and the PowerShell script used to configure it. Also, it identifies assemblies and version numbers, using precisely the same name that will appear in a SharePoint features list, on the file system or in the global assembly cache.
- Dependent services: These are the services upon which SharePoint Services rely.
- Service configuration: These are the SharePoint Services configuration changes that are required.
- SharePoint features created: This lists each new **Site Collection** and **Site Features** that this solution creates.
- Dependent features: This is a list of each feature that needs to be activated/deactivated or configured in order for this solution to operate. It identifies whether this gets done manually, by script, or by code.
- Source artifacts: This lists each source artifact and its location.
- IIS: This lists each change to IIS needed/made by this solution.
- The web configuration file: This documents all changes needed/made to the `web.config` file.

- Feature ID/GUID: This lists each feature ID or GUID that was created for our solution.

Please note the same SPSG works for in-house or outsourced custom solutions, as well as, purchased solutions.

You will have to decide which solution needs to be SPSG applied. Obviously a trivial solution like moving web parts around on a page is not required because these only require configuration, but pretty much any solution that involves customization (using a high-level tool) or coding (programming) certainly is a candidate for this documentation.

 For the SharePoint hardcore folks; SharePoint could be thought of as a repository for these documents, because of the version control and content approval functionality, but thinking about Disaster Recovery, it is entirely likely that these documents might not be available when we need them the most.

If SharePoint is the repository, make sure that your team has up-to-the-minute access to your documents; be sure to synchronize them with a SharePoint Workspace, a local drive, or at the very least connect the library to your Outlook and place a copy there.

A great new feature in SharePoint 2013 is **SkyDrive Pro**. SkyDrive Pro allows you to store documents on your personal site content library, while keeping them synchronized with a desktop folder. We would never want DR documents to be hidden on some individual's desktop, especially during a disaster. Consider creating a user called "Disaster Manager", give her a laptop that sits in your remote business continuity site, and use SkyDrive Pro to keep those documents synchronized with that laptop. From there, you have many options to access, reproduce, and synchronize with others. This is discussed in *Chapter 8, Disaster Recovery Techniques for End Users.*

Another practical idea is to store all deployed solutions on a well-advertised network share, and map it over to your SharePoint Front End server, something like `Z:\SPSolutions` where each solution package is contained in a separate folder, for example, `Z:\SPSolutions\CustomWebPart1`. In restore cases, where solutions require redeployment, they will be easy to locate.

Change Management and SharePoint

Change Management as defined by any of the IT service management standards such as ITIL or MOF, is a very well defined process. The challenge with SharePoint is that the platform is constantly changing. The users are always adding content, new libraries, new sites, new collections, as well as modifying list, site, site collection, and farm settings. To say SharePoint is always changing is not the least bit of an exaggeration.

This constant state of change does put some pressure on any Change Management process, and you will need to adapt your SharePoint Change Management process to your compliance requirements. Here are a few good starting points.

The standard

No change to the production or staging farm is ever permitted without first completing the appropriate **Change Management Process**.

At face value, the "standard" might seem outrageous or impossible, but it's not. Every organization needs to clearly define which change requires a **Change Request**, and what the exceptions are. The following two lists provide a starting point.

Changes requiring a Change Request:

- Farm changes performed using Central Admin, PowerShell or STSADM
- Web App create/delete using Central Admin, PowerShell or STSADM
- Web App configuration settings using Central Admin, PowerShell or STSADM
- Site collection configuration settings using site collection settings, PowerShell or STSADM
- Site customizations using SharePoint Designer or InfoPath Designer.
- Restore using Central Admin, PowerShell or STSDAM
- Import using Central Admin, PowerShell or STSDAM
- All other farm/server/application recovery
- Operating system patches
- Deployment of all centrally-administered solutions using Central Admin, PowerShell or STSADM

- Deployment of all sandboxed solutions using site collection settings, PowerShell or STSADM
- Content added/deleted/changed using automated tools or scripts
- Site and content changes using manage sites and structure
- Configuration of diagnostic logs outside of emergency incident response

The following are changes not requiring a Change Request:

- Site create/delete
- Site feature active/deactivate
- Site settings
- Site collection create/delete
- Site feature activate/deactivate
- Site collection settings
- Content added/deleted/changed manually
- Site Admin actions
- End user actions
- Backup using Central Admin, PowerShell or STSDAM
- Export using Central Admin, PowerShell or STSDAM
- Configuration of diagnostic logs as needed during emergency incident response

Source code control

Regardless of your software engineering methodology (for example, Scrum, Agile, Extreme), there should be some source control system. Whether you use Source Safe, Microsoft Team Foundation Server, or open source GIT, you need to have something in place. Even using a network drive is far better than leaving your code on the development box upon which it was initially written.

For anything practical, you will be doing your coding and debugging on a SharePoint Farm. Now if your team is large, you will have lots of farms with code scattered about. I will not take up your time reviewing all of the possible issues that you may face when you can't easily find the latest version of your code, but it suffices to say – practice source control!

Another use of a source code control system is to store those artifacts created at the customization level, for example, Visio Diagrams and Access MDB.

The software development life cycle

You might think that a section on the SDLC in a Disaster Recovery book seems a bit out of place, but consider this. If all your customizations are well tested and have been deployed multiple times, how much easier will it be when a crisis occurs? If custom solutions are tested on farms that are configured identical to **Production**, odds are in favor that they'll work in production. Most importantly, if you maintain these supporting farms properly, in a pinch, you can always try a restoration to a **Test** or **Staging** farm before attempting a restore to production.

So what does the SDLC look like? Essentially, every organization should expect to maintain four SharePoint farms, if they do any sort of development. The farms should look like the following:

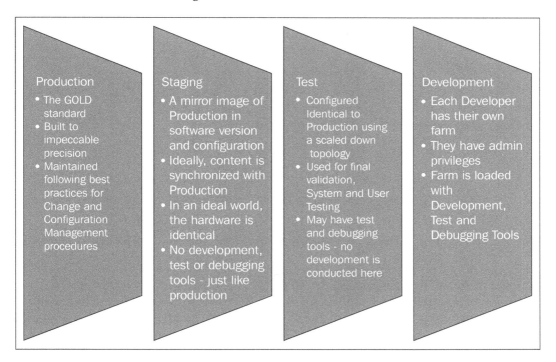

Of course, farms multiply like rabbits, pretty quickly. Since you need a farm for each developer, lots of developers mean lots of farms. It is therefore not uncommon to have more than one Test farm too, for example, testing a new third party solution for end users, while the operations team wants to practice disaster recovery procedures.

All these farms dictate that you have a robust Virtual Server environment and you've put in the time to learn how to spin up a new farm quickly. Of course, if you're capable of doing this for development and testing purposes, in a crisis, you could do the same to restore production.

 Don't have spare hardware or virtual machines? Microsoft can help!

As an alternative to maintaining virtual development farms, each developer can utilize their MSDN subscription, and get their own Office 365 or Azure farm.

Developing for Office 365 (SharePoint 2013) reduces some options available to on-premises, yet any solution developed for Office 365 will run on-premises.

Your MSDN subscription provides credits and discounts that may be applied to Azure Cloud Virtual Machines. Essentially, you can pay Microsoft to host your development farm.

While we're talking about Microsoft cloud services, take a look at Team Foundation Service. Microsoft is offering five accounts on a hosted TFS platform. As of this writing it, too, is free with an MSDN subscription:

`http://msdn.microsoft.com/en-us/subscriptions/aa718661.aspx`

 Practice makes perfect, as the saying goes.

Maintain consistency across your Development, Test, Staging and Production farms.

At this point of the chapter you can see that the production and supporting farms in their environment that has consistency in the configuration between each farm is a key discipline to maintain. The truth is that each really needs to be configured identically, or any testing will be based on uncontrolled variables. At minimum, we need to ensure that each farm has the same services configured in the same way, using identical (or exactly the same) service accounts. The IIS Application Pools must be configured identically and every other setting in central administration should also be the same.

While managing all of these farms implies a competency with virtual machines and SharePoint system administration; the best starting place is to have clearly defined standards, and a repeatable installation procedure supported by accurate documentation.

The time you take to work these out up front will pay huge dividends down the road.

There is one exception to our rigorous standards and that is Development farms. The challenge we face is maintaining control while allowing our developers to innovate and leverage new services and features (that is possibly not being used in PROD), after all, isn't that the point of solution development to use the capabilities of the platform whenever it makes sense. This problem is easily solved with a little bit of discipline and the **SharePoint Solution Governance** (**SPSG**) document discussed earlier in this chapter.

From the start of the design phase, and throughout the development cycle, the developer needs to document addition and changes to services and features. This way, when the solution is turned over for testing, "drift" from the current production configuration is well-known.

How to use supporting farms

Using supporting farms effectively is fairly straightforward. Let's start with defining what is a supporting farm. In short, it is anything that is not hosting production content or applications. Supporting farms refers to the collection of farms used to support the SharePoint **Application Lifecycle Management** (**ALM**) process.

To learn more about SharePoint ALM and the specific terminology Microsoft users refer to the Application Lifecycle Management in SharePoint 2010:

`http://msdn.microsoft.com/en-us/library/gg604045(v=office.14).aspx`

Development is performed on a development farm where the developer conducts his research and development, writes, and debugs his application, and packages up the solution. In classic software engineering terms, the development farm is a place where unit testing is conducted. Before the solution can be delivered for "integration/system" test to a Test farm, the deployment package has to include the SPSG document, installation instructions (which include configuration instructions), scripts, and the solution package itself. All of the artifacts are properly stored in the correct locations (source control, shared folders, Team Foundation Server, and so on).

Please be sure that before the developer hands-off the package, it is deployed at least once on a development farm from Central Admin, Solution Management, or add an application page.

 Using Visual Studio's **Deploy Solution** button to deploy a solution does not exercise the same user interfaces, and will not give the developer "the other guy's perspective". In this case, the other guy is a poor system administrator who might have to redeploy this solution during a crisis.

Ideally the deployment package is handed off to another team member other than the developer to deploy to the Test farm. This ensures that the instructions are clear, and all the bits work without having a deep knowledge of the solution. With the deployment package in the predetermined location (for example, `Z:\SPSolutions\newsolution`), the solution can be deployed.

Once deployed, even before testing the new functionality, you must first validate that only the features and services identified in the SPSG were affected. This is the right time to refine the documentation if it is anything less than 100 percent accurate. Expect to iterate a few times moving from Development to Test, or maybe more than a few times.

Once testing is 100 percent successful, the Staging farm deployment can occur. But prior to this, two things should happen:

- Production content should be synced to the Staging farm, so that we have an up-to-date test environment. This is important not only because we really want the latest version of some document, but also we need to ensure that we have all of the configuration and customization changes, which get stored in content databases, or else we're not going to get a "production-like" validation.

- Staging is treated just like Production, and follows our Change Request (CR) procedures. If your organization does not practice some form of change management, I strongly suggest that you do it for SharePoint, as discussed earlier in this chapter.

After everything is validated on Staging, submit the Change Request for the production deployment and go live.

This methodology will work every time because of the following reasons:

1. You have properly and identically configured the farms.

2. You have deployed the solution in the exact same way a few times already; the law of averages dictates that you'll get it right by the time you get to Production.

Developing configuration dependencies needed for your solution

It is not always possible — or practical — to code-in configuration changes. Sometimes it is just plainly easier to launch a browser and change a few settings. The problem with this approach is that the little details will be forgotten in the heat of a restore process, such as: Who could possibly remember that our little employee Time-off Request had Content Approval turned on in the library? And to be totally realistic, even with copious documentation most operations teams do not have the luxury of time when a restore becomes necessary.

There are two simple ways to handle a constant:

- For each solution you develop, start by writing a simple set of instructions describing how to deploy the solution. These instructions should describe all the "manual" steps that are needed before and after the deployment or its use.

- Follow up with a PowerShell script which automates these manual steps. The documentation provides the knowledge, while the script makes it repeatable, arguably with less opportunity for human error.

SharePoint 2013 App Development Model

Until now, this chapter has concentrated on the farm solution model with which most of the readers are familiar. With SharePoint 2013, Microsoft has introduced the Cloud App Model. There are excellent resources on MSDN and other sites that explain the pros and cons in detail, but it is necessary to understand the fundamental difference and the impact on our Disaster Recovery procedures.

The Cloud App Model essentially requires applications that may be hosted on one of the following three places:

- A hosting provider

- Auto-hosted using Windows Azure and SQL Azure

- SharePoint hosted

This cloud model is illustrated in the following figure:

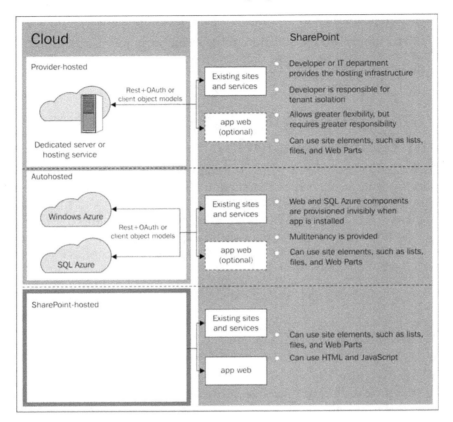

 The Apps for SharePoint overview and MSDN Library can be found at:
`http://msdn.microsoft.com/en-us/library/fp179930.aspx`

While the Cloud App Model is clearly needed to support the Microsoft App Store, the real power is realized when building SharePoint applications that can take advantage of Microsoft Azure on-demand computer power or **Platform as a Service (PaaS)**. While it is entirely possible to expand your on-premises SharePoint farm by deploying additional App tier servers, the cost and complexity of doing so can become a bit daunting. The same goes for provider-hosted alternatives. In fact, any time you have to pre-build computing capacity, you have a less desirable cost per CPU cycle ratio. The power of spinning up a multiple computing threads as the demand dictates, while only paying for the time that the processes are actually running is a very intoxicating prospect for any developer.

As developers, we now have the ability to build applications that do not burden farms, while leveraging incredible scaling potential. Even if you don't take advantage of Microsoft Azure PaaS, you're still likely to create "apps" that rely upon external data or computing power. While we might have some external dependencies today, for example, an RSS Feed source or an online web service, the introduction of the Cloud App Model for SharePoint will accelerate the consumption of external services as we see new innovations around the new App Model. It will be an inevitable part of every SharePoint environment.

A dependency on external services can be both a benefit and a detriment to a Disaster Recovery procedure. In a full-system Disaster Recovery scenario, where the entire production environment is required to come up in the DR facility, it is likely that the external system(s), upon which we're dependent, didn't skip a beat. If our interface to them is simplistic, it is likely that the service will just pop up on the new DR farm. Unfortunately, it is more likely that security considerations will come into play. How the external service resolves the authentication, and how it may rely on certificates or IP addresses, will affect whether our DR site will be able to easily consume the service during the recovery cycle.

Taking advantage of the Cloud App Model necessarily has to call into play the additional network planning steps as during the software design phase, which will impact Disaster Recovery. In fact, it will likely influence our choices as developers, when it comes to authentication or security considerations.

Most developers at some time have faced security challenges when doing any sort of system integration. Unique to SharePoint development is simply that these challenges will come up very often under the Cloud App Model. This will be another case of forward thinking going a very long way.

The Cloud App Model will also drive a need to consider the external providers' SLA. If our requirements call for a specific restore time or an annual uptime requirement, can our external provider meet that requirement? I think it is simply phenomenal that Microsoft Azure has such confidence in their datacenter investments that they can offer a 99.9 percent uptime guarantee, but this won't be enough, if our internal requirements demand anything more than 99.95 percent.

While service level concerns are not typically the domain of the corporate IT developer, the Cloud App Model will force the developer to take a holistic look at the overall architecture and recoverability. In fact, cloud computing in general forces developers to consider how they modularize their code, reduce overhead, and recover from errors.

To leave you with one point from the Cloud App Model; it is that cloud computing changes the game, relies on external resources, and the particular details of each application must be considered in our Disaster Recovery plans.

JavaScript and jQuery – where do they go?

Earlier in the chapter we discussed including JavaScript and jQuery in our source control system as a basic development requirement. Perhaps a more important consideration is how these get deployed in the first place. Embedded scripts can go unnoticed or unaccounted for, making it easy to overlook them during a recovery.

In SharePoint 2010 it is a common practice to embed JavaScript right into a content editor web part, its fast, easy, and the code travels with the content database. This is illustrated in the following figure. The problem with this technique is that the code (JavaScript) is obscured, and nobody may realize it's even there. This makes it much harder to track and maintain. In case of any content recovery, it's also possible that the version of code gets out of sync with the content.

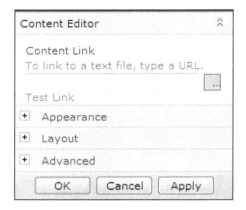

Some improvements were made in SharePoint 2013 that really helps. We now have a Script Editor web part. As the name implies, this web part's role is to host scripts. Knowing that this web part is used on a page provides immediate indication that the page contains script code. This is a big benefit over using the Content Editor web part, which we simply didn't know if contained code or just content.

Another helpful improvement, aside from being able to do some really cool content interaction is the **JS Link** available for most list and library app parts.

The JS Link points to a file which contains script code which will be called in a pre or post render. If you are careful, you'll put all your JS Links in a single place, and maintain those scripts using your source control system.

Using files rather than embedding script directly, makes it much easier to maintain the code independently of the content. In the case of a disaster recovery, it's a pretty simple matter of restoring a bunch of text files.

Designing with Disaster Recovery in mind

There are as many techniques to follow as there are languages, frameworks, and development with which to implement them. When it comes to SharePoint, what is most important is to clearly understand the underlying features and services upon which you're relying, and how they react during a single point of failure or a full-blown farm failure.

A simple navigational element like a little JavaScript button that merely opens another .ASPX page might not be impacted during a failover situation, but a solution which has a major Feature or Service dependency might be an entirely different matter.

Let's look at a common scenario, a simple custom Search web part that returns a list of customers and their contact information. Search is a powerful service that can easily be leveraged to a little point solution, as mentioned. In fact, in SharePoint 2013, Microsoft now provides a Search web part and a display template framework just to help designers use the service without larger development investments. But I digress!

Now back to our solution. To ensure that your solution will work predictably during DR you have to ask three simple but critical questions:

- Does my solution rely on a service which might not be immediately available during a disaster recovery failover?
- How will the loss of this service affect my solution?
- Will it cause my solution to yield incorrect results?

Using our Search web part solution let's answer each question. The first question is easy in this case; yes, we need Search to be working. Now let's qualify what "working" means. Search working not only means the service is running, but also that the appropriate Index, Content Source and Content Scope (2010) or Result Queries (2013) are working as well.

How will the loss of service affect my solution? To answer that, you will want to test the solution and see what happens when each of the qualifying conditions is not met.

Meaning, what happens when the Service, Index, Content Source/Result Query is not working. While you're at it, do not forget to test the various permutations. Mathematically it means you have a lot of testing to do!

To answer the last question, you will want to look at those conditions that "appear" to work, and validate whether they in fact return the correct data. It surely can't be considered working if the wrong data is returned. In our example, imagine the embarrassment when we contact customer A to discuss customer B's issue.

Now that we have a firm grasp on our results. We need to speak with the DR team and understand their plans for restoring not just the farm, but my dependent service as well. Search is a particularly good service to illustrate, because it is easy to make Search a low priority for restoration. After all how important is it to find that five year old PowerPoint file? Also, it is not uncommon or terribly bad decision, not to restore the Search index database when you can easily just run a new one. Makes sense, except that it takes time to run, and now my solution might be vulnerable during that time.

After aligning with the DR team and plan, now you want to consider improvements in your code, making it a bit more fail-safe. It is fairly easy to check if a service is running, and not a whole lot of effort to see if some other required component is available, before we execute our logic. Coding in feature and service checks will make your code much more resilient. It is far better to display "Dependent Service (Search) Unavailable, try again later" rather than returning incorrect data or a cryptic exception, especially during a crisis.

Using the DR site for testing

 Let me start with this – don't do it! Mucking around with the DR site, deliberately causing the configuration to drift from the Production farm will not make things easier during a crisis.

Using the DR site for testing introduces risk and questions the reliability of our DR farm; will it actually work when it is time to execute our DR procedures? Using DR for testing is definitely not a best practice, and it definitely will not help you sleep well at night.

Unfortunately, budget constraints and poor decision making might force you to work this way. If you must do this, at least introduce some standards that give you a fighting chance when disaster strikes.

Do not ever do development using primary web application URLs or Port Numbers! Web apps tend to proliferate and it's much easier to avoid mistakes when you clearly separate production from non-production web apps.

Assuming your default Web application are using port numbers, as a recommended best practice (for example, `http://portal::29765`) do not accept random defaults. Instead, use a well-defined range for production applications and use a different range for their development equivalents. Follow the same standard on all Development, Testing and Staging farms too. While you're at it, use the same portal for Central Administration on all your farms too.

Here is a start for your standard

Please refer the following table for the production port assignments

Web Application	Port Number
Central Administration	1025
Mysite	8080
1st Web App	8081
2nd Web App	8082
3rd Web App	8083

Please refer the following table for the development port assignments

Web Application	Port Number
Central Administration	1025
Mysite	9090
1st Web App	9091
2nd Web App	9092
3rd Web App	9093

Clearly separating Development web apps and Production web apps will keep production undisturbed, to a degree. Of course using Alternate Access Mapping will allow you to create user-friendly URLs.

Keeping web apps separate is good for data and customizations, since they get stored within a content database, but won't prevent a farm-based solution from messing up production. To manage this situation, the developer has to take on a bit more responsibility and leverage Assembly Versioning.

While it is a common practice by all commercial (Microsoft) and corporate developers to reuse assembly version numbers (just look at the GAC and see how many are 1.0.0.0), if you are going to mix new development with production, you have to facilitate multiple versions of the same code and assembly version numbers. This does create a more administrative burden, since Web Configuration Safe Control and Master Page Delegate Control entries will be different for production and development software. There are a number of ways to handle this, each with their own considerations, but recognizing that you have the burden and addressing it may help you to meet your DR requirement.

The hive

You will have to deal with files in the hive. Again, this is tied to versioning and you will probably just start keeping multiple folders—one for each version. Eventually, you will realize that, while designing, you will have to put as much care into the upgrade or redeployment of a solution as the initial installation and deployment. The "what happens when I have to upgrade a piece of my solution" use case, is a worthy consideration, regardless of your DR procedures or environment.

Pulling it all together

All of these procedures might seem a little daunting, but looking at the following figure we can see that it really is not so complex:

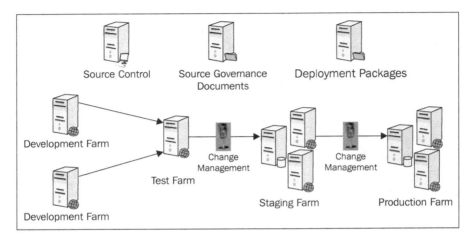

So far we can conclude that the previous section has been describing procedural steps, which can be performed, to run a reliable environment. So how does this this help during a restoration?

All of the steps described earlier really position the development staff to be able to support virtually any sort of crisis or recovery scenario because:

- We know where all our solutions are located and can easily mount them for redeployment
- We're certain the latest versions have been published
- We have solid documentation to support redeployment if necessary
- We have our source artifacts in a source control system and can always recreate a solution, in a worst case scenario

Now that we have a governance procedure in place and the releases are starting to follow some "common-sense" development practices, it is time to consider the role of the developer during the recovery process.

The role of the developer during recovery

At face value, the developer might seem unnecessary as part of the Disaster Recovery team. Isn't a production outage an operations issue?

 Carefully planned Disaster Recovery procedures executed with Swiss-watch precision by our outstanding operations team, should keep the development team free of any recovery responsibility. Nothing could be further from the truth.

Even when everything goes as planned; the role of the developer should be to execute the application test plans before any other user ever tries. The fact is that the developer should be closer to the user. After all, they understood enough about the business requirements to develop the application in the first place. Not to mention, they developed unit, system and user acceptance test plans during development and stabilization phases, so who better to ensure that the application or customization is running as designed on the Disaster farm.

Assuming you agree with my simple logic, having access to test plans and any test automation used to execute those plans will be critical during a disaster. Very often in complex DR plans, testing the recovered system is overlooked or rationalize that just being up is good enough. This might have been true in the early years, when SharePoint was exclusively a collaboration platform, but as SharePoint has evolved to become a class-A business system hosting mission critical applications; it must be treated just like any other critical line of business system.

To streamline the testing process, it will be helpful to classify customizations and application by priority to the business and to the platform. For example, the employee-shopping cart where employees go to buy company goods at a discount may not be very important during a disaster. On the other hand, that little custom navigation control that has become the only way you can navigate between major applications might appear small, but may just cripple usability if missing in action.

Now that we have made the developer a key player in the recovery process, what happens when our development staff is also affected by the disaster?

In 2012, Hurricane Sandy, which hit New York and New Jersey particularly hard, clearly demonstrated what happens when a broad geographical area is affected by a common disaster. The first instinct is to place your DR site several zones away, but Sandy took down electrical power for weeks; many people could not work from home. It created fuel shortages, and shut down mass transit systems, making transportation impossible. In fact, New York City shut down bridges and tunnels for the first 48 hours, essentially cutting off egress from or to Long Island.

It is imperative that our test plans are not only available during a crisis but executable by personnel other than the development team. This means cross training staff, maybe even enlisting the end user community and empowering them with new skills and tools. For sure, automated testing becomes paramount — "just press this button and read the results here, if it's green you're good to go", should be the objective we aim for.

If you conclude that a developer's involvement in the Disaster Recovery process starts way before development of an application ever begins, you have been paying attention. Congratulate yourself with your favorite beverage.

Sure you have a role to play during the actual disaster, but the effort that goes into how you develop, architect, design and deploy your solutions may turn out to be much more important during a crisis.

Summary

This chapter has introduced you to the DR for custom development for SharePoint 2013.

Clearly, there is definitely a need here for a tool or maybe the mother of all PowerShell scripts to make this procedure easier, but until that appears, documentation, discipline, and some well-defined procedures will go a very long way during a crisis.

This chapter has set the stage so that you understand and be aware of, for planning and DR plan to support their SharePoint deployment.

The following chapter explains how to perform testing and maintenance on a DR environment so the administrator has the confidence that the documentation is actually workable.

In the next chapter, recovery of content for end users is explained.

8
Disaster Recovery Techniques for End Users

This chapter explains data prevention and recovery procedures that should be applied by users with their SharePoint collaboration activities to prevent data loss.

The reader of this book is probably technical, and therefore perhaps a little surprised by the title and the topic of this chapter. You probably assume that DR is an IT department activity, so why should the end user even think about it?

 Well this DR concept is wrong and might work in the mainframe world, but with SharePoint, the approach should be "we are all in this together".

Financially, this approach makes sense as well. The following screenshot shows the SharePoint costs for 1,000 users over a 3-year period. If IT support can be reduced by just 2 percent through end user education, the savings would equate to almost $40,000, by not doing a lot of extra work. Unfortunately, this is often overlooked, because there is a perception that end users already have SharePoint knowledge.

Approximate number of users	1000
Hardware	$352,974.99
Software	$265,415.70
People	$1,932,000.00
Outsourcing	$235,000.00
Total cost of SharePoint over 3 years	$2,785,390.69

Source: www.huddle.com

In the previous screenshot, the people costs are manpower such as support, administration, trainers, and development.

In this chapter, we will cover the following points:

- Why end user DR training is often forgotten
- Useful end user DR practices
- Managing expectations
- Training

Why is end user DR training often forgotten?

Why is end user DR training often forgotten? End user DR is often overlooked by the IT department because typical DR procedures involve SQL Server backup plans, server images, and third-party backup tools, all of which are handled by IT resources. End users are not necessarily technical and are not accustomed to performing even the simplest backup and restore procedures.

When IT puts together a DR plan, the procedures normally focus on the "big hairy" disasters which are costly, highly visible to upper management, and effort large user communities. The small end user issues are often overlooked. These small issues are more common than one would think.

 Often, IT's perception of end users is that they are not capable of protecting their content with scheduled backups and although this is often the case, you can set up a DR process targeted to the end users.

Although end users usually only manipulate content, it is the deleted content, such as sites, files, and list items that is most alarming to them. These end user *disasters* have their own negative effect on productivity and business continuity.

Useful end user DR practices

This section explains simple, yet often overlooked SharePoint functionality that enables the end user to recover content without the IT helpdesk number being dialed.

Recycle bins

Often an end user will delete content and not realize this information can be retrieved from the end user site recycle bin.

To retrieve content from the end user site recycle bin, follow these steps:

1. In the quick launch tray, click on **Site Contents**, as shown in the following screenshot:

2. Select **Recycle Bin** on the ribbon, as shown in the following screenshot:

3. Choose the file that you wish to restore, and then select the **Restore Selection** link, as depicted in the following screenshot:

The file will be restored to the original location from where it was deleted. This simple and easy activity can be performed by the end user.

 By default, content stays in the recycle bin for 30 days and then it is moved to the Site Collection's recycle bin.

The **Site Collection Administrator** can also restore content at the top-level site of the Site Collection by selecting the **Recycle bin** on the Site Content page.

The following screenshot explains the first and second stage recycle bins:

Site Collection Administration
Recycle bin
Search Result Sources
Search Result Types
Search Query Rules
Search Schema
Search Settings
Search Configuration Import
Search Configuration Export
Site collection features
Site hierarchy
Site collection audit settings
Audit log reports
Portal site connection

One of the advantages of the Site Collection administrator or IT performing this activity is that they do not need to navigate to the actual site where the document was deleted. This makes the restore process slightly quicker.

 This recycle bin restore feature can save the day, because often senior committees often meet once a month—every 30 days—just when deleted content is being moved to the Site Collection recycle bin, which requires a Site Collection administrator's intervention. So it makes sense to extend the duration of the site recycle bin.

Increase the site recycle bin retention time

Problem

An executive level committee meets once a month, at the end of the month. The default site recycle bin configuration moves the deleted items to the second stage (or Site Collection) recycle bin every 30 days (that is, at the end of the month). The committee members are looking to restore deleted content, but find the site recycle bin empty. Due to bad timing, the content was moved to the Site Collection recycle bin right about the time of their monthly meeting! The committee will have to contact the helpdesk to restore the content.

Resolution

Increase the site recycle bin retention time so that it does not coincide with the end-of-month activities.

To extend the duration of the recycle bin, follow the next given steps. This must be performed by someone with the appropriate permissions.

In Central Administration, perform the following steps:

1. Select the web application containing the Site Collection.
2. Click on the **General Settings** button from the ribbon.
3. Select the **General Settings** submenu.

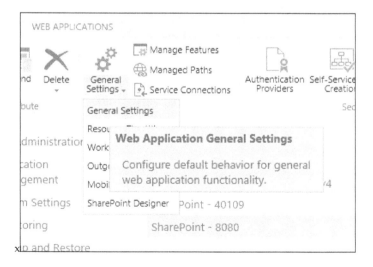

4. Scroll down to the **Recycle Bin** section.

Recycle Bin

Specify whether the
Recycle Bins of all of the
sites in this web
application are turned on.
Turning off the Recycle
Bins will empty all the
Recycle Bins in the web
application.

The second stage Recycle
Bin stores items that end
users have deleted from
their Recycle Bin for easier
restore if needed. Learn
about configuring the
Recycle Bin.

Recycle Bin Status:
  ◉ On   ○ Off
Delete items in the Recycle Bin:
  ◉ After [30] days
  ○ Never
Second stage Recycle Bin:
  ◉ Add [50] percent of live site quota for
second stage deleted items.
  ○ Off

 Only a Site Collection administrator can restore
content in the Site Collection recycle bin.

5. Make the changes to the retention days of the Recycle Bin.

Checked in but not published

Often, end users will upload a document to SharePoint, check it in, but not publish it. This results in restricted visibility to the document for other users, because the document is not published.

The unpublished document is not visible to other end users, so the end user train of thought is that SharePoint is not working and they of course call the help desk.

To prevent this from occurring, educating the end user is key. You will need to explain that the document needs to be published for readership to occur.

 Keeping documents unpublished allows only users with editable access to the content. This might be by design.

The following screenshot illustrates how to publish a document. This also applies to any SharePoint content such as calendar event, or an announcement.

The previous screenshot can be accessed from a view of a list or library and through the item drop-down menu.

Permission

Similar to the previous point of major publishing, an end user unintentionally changes the permission on content and restricts the ability for other users to view or edit it. This is often interpreted as "There's a problem with SharePoint!"

This can be resolved easily with the end user or IT confirming the content permissions by performing the following steps:

1. Open the menu option of the content.

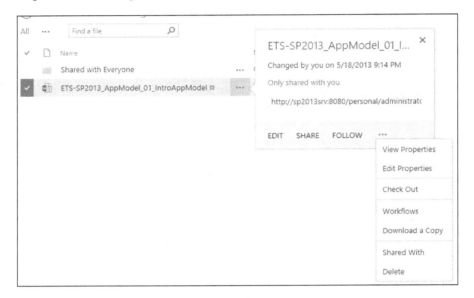

2. Click on **View Properties**.
3. Click on **Share With** on the ribbon.

4. Click on **Advanced**.

5. Select the **Check Permissions** icon.

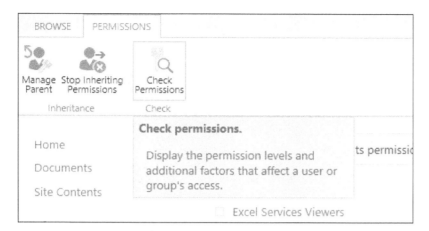

This will confirm who has access to the content.

Users can't remember where their file is saved

This is a common issue with end users, and a call to the Help Desk often follows. Before pulling out the backup and restore documentation, performing a SharePoint search to locate the file could be the quickest way to locate it.

Version control

The version control capabilities of SharePoint are a big selling point of the product that is often overlooked in an actual SharePoint deployment.

 By default, version control is turned off on lists and libraries. Therefore, as a result, previous versions of the document are not recoverable.

To restore a previous version of a content object, carry out the following procedure:

1. Open the menu option of the content.

2. Select **Version History**.

3. Restore a previous version.

 Version history is not turned on automatically when a list/library is created. This is done in the list/library settings, and has to be done for each list/library.

SkyDrive Pro

SkyDrive Pro (Sky Drive) is a Dropbox-type desktop application for the professional community. Files are saved on the end user's PC and synchronized both with other devices and on your My Site SharePoint server. SkyDrive Pro is a part of Office 2013 Standard or ProPlus. It can be installed separately for previous editions of Office, but there is no synchronization client for Office 2010 or 2007.

SkyDrive Pro is similar to the SharePoint Workspace 2010, which was Groove, the Microsoft client software that never really took off. This is mentioned as a comparison of technologies in different versions of SharePoint.

To synchronize files, carry out the following steps:

1. In the document library on your My Site (or any site), click on the **SkyDrive** link on the menu as shown in the following screenshot:

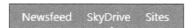

This will display the following screen:

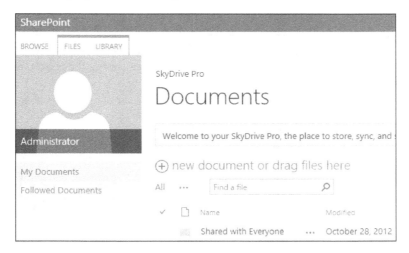

2. Click on the **SYNC** link on the ribbon (top right-hand corner).

The content in the library and the end user's desktop will be synchronized.

This is an end user DR procedure if the SharePoint server is unavailable. The files can be stored offline are still accessible.

Admittedly, this is a temporary measure, but it still provides content workability for the end user.

 This is not peer-to-peer software, so you will need SharePoint in the mix somewhere.

 You can think of SkyDrive Pro as your SkyDrive for business. When you store your files on SkyDrive Pro, only you can see them, but you can easily share them with co-workers and access them from your mobile devices. Your files are safely kept in the cloud with SharePoint Online, or on your company's SharePoint Server 2013 servers, depending on what your company has set up.

Microsoft's SkyDrive was previously called Windows Live SkyDrive and Windows Live Folders is a file hosting service that allows users to upload and synchronize files to cloud storage and then access them from a web browser or their local device.

It is part of the Windows Live range of online services, and allows users to keep their files private, share them with contacts, or make the files public.

This is a consumer-based file storage service available through your Microsoft account.

SkyDrive, not SkyDrive Pro, has no relationship to SharePoint Server 2013. However, if you install Office 2013 and open Windows Explorer, you see a SkyDrive folder in the favorites section.

For more information regarding SkyDrive, visit the following links:

- `http://technet.microsoft.com/en-us/library/dn167720.aspx`
- `http://office.microsoft.com/en-us/word-help/share-a-document-using-sharepoint-or-skydrive-HA102849692.aspx`

- `http://community.office365.com/en-us/forums/154/t/162276.aspx`
- `http://sharepoint.microsoft.com/Blogs/GetThePoint/Lists/Posts/Post.aspx?ID=675`
- `http://sharepoint.microsoft.com/blog/Pages/BlogPost.aspx?pID=1015`
- `http://sharepoint.microsoft.com/blog/Pages/BlogPost.aspx?pID=1033`
- `http://community.office365.com/en-us/blogs/office_365_technical_blog/archive/2013/05/29/skydrive-pro-client-for-windows-now-available.aspx`

By implementing the previous practices, the urgent support calls and the "Let me walk over to your desk" activity of the day should be reduced.

Managing end user expectations

End user and business expectations must be managed. This is in line with what is stated in *Chapter 1, Planning and Key Concepts – What Not to Forget*, along with service level agreements. When there is a problem, how does it get resolved and how quickly is the business, IT, and user community made aware of the recovery time? Is there a support number to call, or is there just an online ticketing system.

 Just because the content is a Microsoft Word document does not mean that it is not important to someone who is important. So SharePoint support needs to be part of helpdesk support.

Training

The points mentioned in this chapter should be covered as part of end user training. The authors cannot stress how important end user training is to the end user DR procedure.

This does not have to be more than an hour for a user, but the payoff is huge for uptime and a working environment for the end user. Cheat sheets are useful to provide tips in resolving easy and simple issues.

Summary

In this chapter the reader has been introduced to several simple techniques that can reduce the support calls or fire drill activities related to end user disaster recovery. These techniques will not save the day if SQL Server crashes, but this activity is not daily support activity to the business.

The SharePoint cost of ownership is not the software licenses but the user support staff. If this can be reduced through user training, then the end user is more productive and IT is freed up.

 From experience, the authors would state, SharePoint 2010 licensing is approximately 5 percent of the total cost, with the remaining 95 percent represented by the administration and support costs.

The following chapter discusses SharePoint DR in the cloud. Cloud DR is an important topic, and should not be overlooked.

9
In the Clouds

As cloud computing matures, an increasing number of organizations are starting to reap the potential benefits and cost savings gained by migrating their applications and IT infrastructures to mainstream cloud providers. In terms of disaster recovery, the cloud can offer significant advantages over traditional approaches by offering rapid provisioning, faster recovery times, and multisite/multi-region availability, at a fraction of the cost of conventional disaster recovery. But just as with traditional DR, there is no one-size-fits-all solution or single blueprint for all to follow. Each firm's requirements are specific, and thus will need to be addressed individually.

Moving SharePoint workloads to the cloud is a hot topic for most CIOs/CTOs, but initial conversations generally center on performance and security; disaster recovery often does not make the first cut. Nonetheless, disaster recovery in the context of cloud environments is a very important topic and should not be overlooked. This chapter aims to clear up any ambiguities about SharePoint, high availability (HA), Disaster Recovery (DR), and the cloud.

In this chapter, you will learn about the following topics:

- DR: on-premise versus cloud
- DR: cloud versus cloud-native
- Common concerns regarding cloud DR
- Cloud responsibility
- General approaches to cloud DR
- Amazon Web Services and HA/DR
- Windows Azure and HA/DR

DR – on-premise versus cloud

The implementation of disaster recovery has significantly evolved in recent times, from tape-based solutions to collocation and hosted services, to cloud computing and managed service offerings. However, unlike previous DR manifestations, cloud computing takes a fully-virtualized approach to disaster recovery by encapsulating all server resources (operating system, patches, applications, data, and so on) into a virtual bundle, which can then be copied or transferred across environments in minutes. This significantly reduces recovery times when compared to conventional DR approaches, where servers needed to be preloaded with the entire stack, including the operating system, prior to initiating data restoration.

The cloud also makes DR cold sites obsolete, as warm or hot sites become a very cost-effective option that can be easily and permanently architected as part of the application architecture, or spun up on-demand. This implementation is a departure from traditional DR, where significant up-front investment was required to even set up the capability for off-site duplication of data and infrastructure, such as facilities, security over assets, suitable capacity, maintenance, and support. Add to that the ease of setting up multisite and multi-region availability (capabilities that where traditionally neglected due to the inherent costs, implementation, and testing challenges), and using the cloud for disaster recovery quickly becomes an attractive alternative.

Along with cloud computing comes **disaster recovery as a service** (**RaaS** or **DRaaS**), predetermined vendor instantiated service offerings that can help organizations realize improved recovery speeds and cost savings through automation and multi-tenancy.

The advent of cloud services coincides with organizations looking to update or renew their disaster recovery practices, and there are many benefits to be gained by integrating DR with the cloud, including the following:

- **Reduced costs**: It introduces no capital expenditures, has predictable usage-based costing, and includes the possibility of subscription-based services

- **Rapid provisioning and recovery**: It covers on-demand infrastructure, optimized resource usage, fine-tuned performance, hardware/software footprint reduction, and strict SLAs guarantee disruptions are kept to a minimum

- **Regular testing**: Multi-site/multi-region scenarios can be easily tested, and temporary infrastructures provisioned on-demand with no impact to production assets

- **Robustness and flexibility**: It covers ease in modifying DR infrastructures/processes based on changing DR plans and business requirements

DR – cloud versus cloud-native

The cloud is still a relatively nascent technology, and explicitly defining the boundaries of what makes an IT concept or service truly a "cloud" construct can be a bit confusing. Anything that runs in the cloud can technically be considered a cloud technology, but that does not mean that it is actually cloud-native, or really taking advantage of what the cloud has to offer. For example, a simple forklift of an on-premise application-oriented disaster recovery solution onto a cloud **infrastructure as a service (IaaS)** platform will result in the solution functioning the same way as it did on-premise — other than the fact that it is now hosted in a public or private cloud. The functionality will essentially remain unchanged, and the difference in implementation is negligible, when comparing the originating physical or virtualized hosting infrastructure and the destination cloud infrastructure. Certain cloud features, such as scalable storage and multi-site support can further augment the implementation, but ultimately it is still a forklift, and an entry-level step into the cloud. Nonetheless, the DR application's new residency technically makes it part of the cloud, and it will likely be perceived as a true 'cloud technology' by decision makers.

Moving beyond application-oriented software, another broad class of cloud disaster recovery solutions are infrastructure-oriented solutions. Infrastructure-oriented DR solutions take it a step further by failing over groups of resources or entire environments as needed. These solutions are intended for enterprise-wide disaster recovery, and are typically application-agnostic. While they can be well positioned for hybrid deployments between datacenters and cloud environments, they are slightly more difficult to integrate within a cloud infrastructure, and are still typically considered a technology forklift rather than an optimized DR process redesigned with the cloud as a driving force.

On the other hand, disaster recovery using a cloud-native approach can fundamentally change an organization's DR roadmap by embracing the cloud's touted benefits: seemingly endless compute capacity, scalability, and elasticity, all outsourced "as a service". This can include simply using cloud storage, or architecting and integrating with specific **platform as a service (PaaS)**, IaaS, or **software as a service (SaaS)** offerings. As mentioned earlier, an increasingly popular option is to leverage DRaaS or to put an organization's DR needs in the hands of a **managed service provider (MSP)**. For many organizations, this not only represents a change in technology, but can also represent a major shift in costing, process, and delivery.

The following figure shows the categories of disaster recovery solutions as they pertain to the cloud, along with sample listings of products and vendors for each:

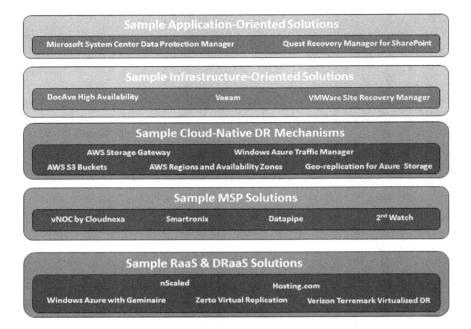

Common concerns regarding cloud DR

SharePoint in the cloud can broadly be defined as the managed, cloud-based delivery of the SharePoint platform, including the underlying server and application infrastructure, network connectivity, security, storage, performance, and potentially licensing services. As mentioned earlier, DR isn't often the first thing that enters the SharePoint and the cloud conversation, but any decision-maker should see how discussing security and performance can easily segue into DR. In fact, when planning a DR strategy, the first items you will likely tackle will deal with both security and performance. Again, there is no one-size-fits-all strategy. The following are a list of common concerns:

- Does my organization have the bandwidth and network capacity to redirect users to the cloud?
- Will my data be secure in transit and at rest in the cloud?

- How will my users be authenticated, and are there provisions for **multi-factor authentication (MFA)**?

- What are my RTO/RPO objectives, and can I maintain them when restoring between infrastructures (for example, from on-premises to the cloud)?

- How prepared are my staff, and how can I test my DR plan?

- Where is the demarcation point in terms of responsibility?

Cloud responsibility

Regarding that last bullet point, it is worth noting that SharePoint 2013 is available in different flavors that can be deployed in a variety of ways with respect to cloud consumption, but this type of deployment and associated integrations can dictate the distribution of responsibility. While most cloud providers typically stress a "shared responsibility" approach to cloud computing, it may be difficult to ascertain the boundaries of that responsibility, which also applies as much to DR as it does to ongoing operations.

Let's take a high-level look at the following three general cloud deployments as they relate to shared responsibility:

- **SaaS**: SharePoint Online is a subscription-based service that provides customers with an enterprise-grade solution for creating websites on which to share documents and information with colleagues and other customers. SharePoint Online is one of several cloud services offered as part of Microsoft Office 365, Microsoft's premiere SaaS offering which, at the time of this writing, has nearly all been converted to SharePoint 2013. This is a great solution for small business or organizations that are looking at "dipping their toe" into cloud usage. Customer responsibility is limited, as the Microsoft ecosystem provides for the majority of administration and management.

- **IaaS**: IaaS leverages virtualization, networking, and storage to build a managed infrastructure for hosting SharePoint. For example, Amazon Web Services (AWS) provides a managed, guaranteed underlying infrastructure, but your organization is wholly responsible for planning, testing, deploying, monitoring, and administering your environment. The same applies to Windows Azure, which recently entered the IaaS market. They can run it, but it's your job to build it and own it. With AWS, Windows Azure (IaaS only), and basically any other IaaS vendor, although 100 percent of your SharePoint infrastructure is hosted in the cloud, the operation and management of that environment is your responsibility.

- **PaaS**: To illustrate SharePoint in relation to PaaS, Windows Azure integrates with SharePoint to service customers through common cloud applications and the extension of on-premise code. Windows Azure (PaaS) is essentially Microsoft's operating system in the cloud. The key difference between Azure (PaaS) and the other cloud options is that it does not involve actually hosting your SharePoint environment. Rather, you are integrating your SharePoint environment with the capabilities offered through Azure in order to provide a richer experience for your end users. This can include reuse of existing Azure services, deploying custom services into the Azure cloud, federating Azure data for search, and so on. With PaaS, the vendor will manage the operating system, middleware and runtime; the applications and data are your responsibility.

This segregation of responsibility between customer and vendor will generally map to how your organization implements DR in the cloud. DRaaS will most closely resemble how SaaS demarcates responsibility, as you are essentially signing up for a managed, packaged service to take care of your resources in an automated fashion. Note that in this case, the process of negotiating appropriate SLAs becomes of utmost importance, as you must be absolutely certain that the provider can deliver uninterrupted service within the defined SLAs. You are, in essence, negotiating access to your data and applications.

The following figure summarizes shared responsibility, as demarcated between vendor and customer, using the main three cloud variants:

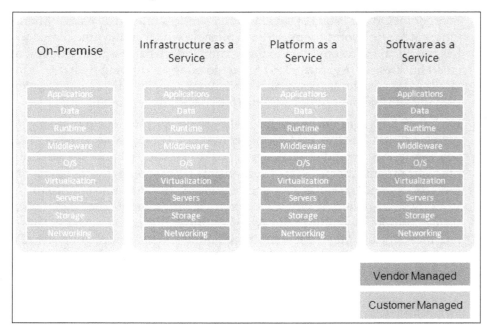

General approaches to cloud DR

Disaster recovery in the cloud has not yet truly been standardized. Anyone that you talk to will have their own conceptual version of an accepted DR model, but the rate of change and evolution of the cloud makes it difficult to effectively standardize and codify an accepted model or process before it gets antiquated. Your best bet is to stop waiting, and to look at what's available to you today, through a variety of different lenses, and examine these options using multiple dimensions and criteria. For example, you can assess disaster recovery methods based on *granularity* — do you want DR at an application level or an infrastructure level? You can gauge your choices based on *effort and responsibility* — do you follow a do-it-yourself (DIY) approach versus a service-oriented approach? Your organization will undoubtedly start their evaluation with *cost*. Then there's *compliance*, or environmental and regulatory constraints that the backup of your applications and data may be subject to. These are just a few criteria to consider.

That said, there are foundational approaches that are generally agreed-upon by most. At a high level, the following will help you to get started in thinking about in what capacity to use the cloud for DR:

- **Backup to the cloud** (restore to on-premise): In this scenario, the primary resources remain on-premise while data is backed up to the cloud. When a disaster occurs, data is restored from the cloud back to on-premise equipment. This scenario is straightforward, and has been around since the beginning of cloud computing. The most challenging aspect of this method has to do with bandwidth limitations when dealing with significant quantities of data. An example product facilitating this approach is AWS Storage Gateway.

- **Replication** (from on-premise to cloud resources): This approach involves the replication of data from source virtual machines (either on-premise or in the cloud) to destination VMs in the cloud. Replication consists of real-time backup and is well suited for applications that require aggressive RTO/RPOs, as well as application awareness. A sample product manifesting this approach is CommVault Continuous Data Replicator.

- **Backup and restore in the cloud**: With this approach, data can originate on- premise, and be backed up into the cloud, but when a disaster occurs, the DR environment is staged in the cloud. Alternatively, the primary environment may already be cloud-native, with disaster recovery also occurring in the cloud, using different sites or regions. This can be implemented by using the suites of services provided by AWS or Windows Azure.

- **Managed Disaster Recovery**: This approach relies on having both production and disaster recovery environments in the cloud, with both being handled by a managed service provider. With this, you are eliminating on-premises infrastructure, taking advantage of usage-based costing, and deferring responsibility to a service provider. This particular market segment has quickly developed from a few providers to hundreds of vendors, with significant growth anticipated in the near future as more companies consider managed services.

The remainder of this chapter takes a more detailed look at implementing disaster recovery and high availability in the cloud by using the tools and services natively available through Amazon Web Services and Windows Azure IaaS.

Amazon Web Services and HA/DR

To get a handle on implementing HA/DR for SharePoint running in AWS, you need to first understand AWS and some of the specific service offerings that are available and relevant to a SharePoint implementation. AWS is a collection of remote computing services that together create a cloud-computing platform. This platform provides a myriad of products in various functional categories, including computing, storage, messaging, content delivery, networking, and so on. But AWS is also characterized as a full IaaS provider, and it is this capability that we would be harnessing for a SharePoint infrastructure. The essential infrastructure components that we would typically utilize for SharePoint HA/DR include the following:

- Global infrastructure – regions and Availability Zones
- Amazon Elastic Compute Cloud (Amazon EC2)
- Amazon Elastic Block Store (Amazon EBS)
- Amazon Virtual Private Cloud (Amazon VPC)
- Elastic Load Balancing (ELB)
- Amazon Route 53

This is not at all an exhaustive list, but it is a starting point for architecting a DR solution. These products would essentially form the backbone for SharePoint, so you need to understand what they do and how your organization can potentially leverage them.

Global Infrastructure – regions and availability zones

AWS is available in multiple regions, each region itself having multiple available zones. Each region is a separate geographic area with isolated locations known as availability zones. Each region is completely independent, while availability zones within a region are engineered to be insulated from failures in other availability zones and provide inexpensive, low latency network connectivity. Your organization can easily choose an appropriate location for a DR site, in addition to the production site(s) where your SharePoint ecosystem is fully deployed. At the time of this writing, AWS is available globally in nine regions (Northern Virginia, Northern California, Oregon, GovCloud, Brazil, Ireland, Singapore, Japan, and Australia) with a combined total of twenty five availability zones. For more information, visit `http://docs.aws.amazon.com/AWSEC2/latest/UserGuide/using-regions-availability-zones.html`.

Amazon Elastic Compute Cloud

Amazon EC2 is the core offering that provides your organization with resizable compute capacity in the Amazon cloud. EC2 is an elastic computing environment that provides you with flexibility in terms of hardware configurations, operating systems, software packages, and so on. Through this service, you can retain complete control over your computing resources, while resting assured that your instances are safely running on, and are guaranteed by, Amazon's computing infrastructure. Whereas server provisioning may have once taken hours or days, your organization can now provision server instances in minutes.

So how do you leverage this for SharePoint? EC2 will be the backbone service that provides your SharePoint server infrastructure, allowing your organization to take advantage of all EC2 capabilities. This includes potentially doing the following:

- Create template server images (called **Amazon Machine Images** or **AMIs**) for the different SharePoint roles, to reduce provisioning complexity, overhead, and for quick backup/restore.

- Scale individual SharePoint servers vertically, by modifying hardware resources on the fly.

- Scale SharePoint servers horizontally, by adding additional server instances for a particular SharePoint role or service application.

- Facilitate redundancy and high availability by distributing server instances between different availability zones within a region, between different national regions, between different global regions, and so on.

- Use EC2 Reserved Instances for your fleet of server instances, which will help to ensure that the capacity you need is available when it is required.

For more information on AWS EC2, visit `http://docs.aws.amazon.com/AWSEC2/latest/UserGuide/concepts.html`.

Amazon Elastic Block Store

Amazon EBS provides persistent storage for Amazon EC2 instances through block level storage volumes. This off-instance storage persists independently from the lifetime of an instance. EBS volumes are highly available and highly reliable, and can be used for boot partitions and as standard storage volumes. EBS snapshots are point-in-time snapshots of data volumes, and can be used to back up volumes attached to SharePoint server instances, containing configuration data, content, databases, and so on. For more information on Amazon EBS, visit `http://docs.aws.amazon.com/AWSEC2/latest/UserGuide/AmazonEBS.html`.

Amazon Virtual Private Cloud

Amazon VPC allows your organization to provision a virtual private cloud on an isolated segment of Amazon's scalable infrastructure, where you can specify and control your own virtual networking topology. Amazon VPC can be used to create a completely independent network solely in the cloud, with public-facing subnets and multiple layers of security. Alternatively, Amazon VPC can be used to extend your on-premise network into the cloud, by creating connectivity between your corporate datacenters and your VPC. Whatever your specific DR requirement or strategy, Amazon VPC is very flexible and can adapt to virtually any scenario. Some sample SharePoint deployments in VPCs include the following:

- A standalone SharePoint deployment hosted in a resource forest in a VPC

- A SharePoint deployment that is connected to and is part of an on-premise domain, but that is hosted in a VPC

- A hybrid SharePoint deployment where some components are physically hosted in a datacenter, while others are deployed in a VPC

- A multi-site architecture with multiple SharePoint farms in different regions

For more information on AWS VPC, visit `http://docs.aws.amazon.com/AmazonVPC/latest/UserGuide/VPC_Introduction.html`.

Elastic Load Balancing

ELB is a method of automatically distributing incoming application traffic across multiple Amazon EC2 server instances. With ELB, your organization can achieve fault tolerance in its applications via health detection, session affinity, security, elastic scaling, and so on. For SharePoint, ELB could be used to do the following:

- Distribute load to role-based server instances in a SharePoint farm
- Create a redundant and highly-available SharePoint farm by distributing incoming traffic across a single Availability Zone or multiple Availability Zones.
- Simplify DR plan execution by pre-allocating ELBs for DNS mapping purposes

For additional information on AWS ELB, visit `http://docs.aws.amazon.com/ElasticLoadBalancing/latest/DeveloperGuide/Welcome.html`.

Amazon Route 53

Route 53 is a scalable DNS web service that provides reliable routing to your AWS infrastructure, or infrastructure hosted outside of AWS. Route 53 lets you configure DNS failover in active-active, active-passive, and mixed configurations in order to improve availability to your SharePoint resources. For additional information on AWS Route 53, visit `http://docs.aws.amazon.com/Route53/latest/DeveloperGuide/Welcome.html`.

Additional AWS Services for DR

As mentioned earlier, Amazon provides an ever-increasing number of products and services. The ones mentioned above will play an immediate part in the design and implementation of DR in your cloud-based SharePoint infrastructure. However, there are additional services that might not have as direct an impact, or that might not be as obvious in your design. In any case, it is good for you to be aware of them, and how they could prove beneficial in your SharePoint environment. These include:

- **Elastic IPs**: These are static IP addresses that enable you to mask instance or Availability Zone failures via address remapping. This can simplify DR plan execution by pre-allocating IP addresses for most critical systems prior to an actual disaster.
- **Amazon CloudFormation**: This potentially gives your organization an easy way to create collections of SharePoint resources configured as templates. These stacks can be launched, stopped, and saved as needed.

- **Amazon Direct Connect**: This helps you to establish a dedicated network connection from your on-premise network to AWS, creating a hybrid SharePoint infrastructure with potential SharePoint DR sites running in the cloud.

- **AWS Storage Gateway**: This connects an on-premise software appliance with cloud-based storage (AWS S3) in order to back up an on-premise SharePoint environment's data to AWS's storage infrastructure.

To review the complete list of current AWS products and services, please visit `http://aws.amazon.com/products/`.

The following diagram illustrates a simplified view of AWS HA/DR components in action, with regard to a typical production SharePoint ecosystem:

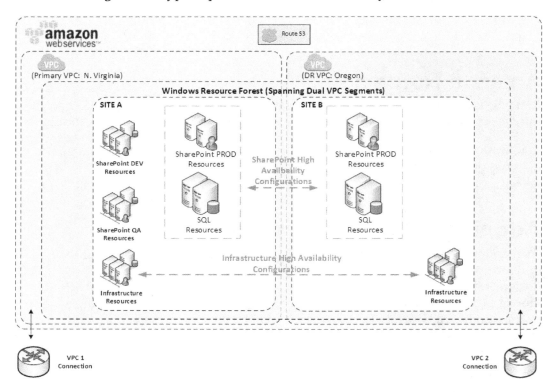

Windows Azure and HA/DR

Microsoft's Windows Azure comes in a few different flavors, but for the purpose of this chapter, we will focus on IaaS components, as they contain the most applicable feature set for SharePoint disaster recovery. Just as with AWS, with Windows Azure you can spin up a SharePoint environment on-demand, and dynamically adjust your usage as needs change. The essential infrastructure components that we would typically utilize for SharePoint HA/DR include the following:

- Global Infrastructure – datacenters and traffic managers
- Virtual network
- Virtual machines
- Load balancing
- Storage
- Hyper-V Recovery Manager

Global infrastructure – datacenters and traffic manager

The Windows Azure cloud maintains datacenters globally, with locations in the United States, Asia, Europe, and soon in Australia and Japan. This enables several disaster recovery scenarios, such as the geo-replication of Windows Azure Storage to secondary datacenters. Currently, there are eight global datacenter locations that can be used to create a complex, distributed SharePoint environment (US East, US West, US North Central, US South Central, Europe West, Europe North, South East Asia, and East Asia).

The Windows Azure Traffic Manager allows your organization to route user traffic to Windows Azure cloud services, regardless of whether they are running in the same datacenter or datacenters in multiple geographic regions. Although it varies in implementation and functionality, this service is somewhat akin to AWS Route 53's DNS failover and AWS ELB. Traffic Manager enables you to automatically manage the failover of user traffic to another datacenter in case the primary datacenter fails. Traffic Manager is also capable of performing load balancing, which is discussed later in this section.

Note that at the time of this writing, Traffic Manager is still in Preview mode. For more information on Windows Azure Traffic Manager visit `http://msdn.microsoft.com/en-us/library/windowsazure/hh744833.aspx`.

Virtual network

The Azure virtual network allows you to provision a logically-isolated section in Windows Azure (similar to AWS VPC) and securely connect it to your on-premise environment. This is ideal for creating a failover environment in the cloud. It also enables the build of distributed SharePoint applications using a hybrid approach, with services being called or data being stored across environments. Windows Azure can be the failover for your physical/virtual datacenter on-premise, or can exclusively act as both the production and disaster recovery site.

For additional information on the Windows Azure Virtual Network, visit http:// msdn.microsoft.com/en-us/library/windowsazure/jj156007.aspx.

Virtual machines

Windows Azure Virtual Machines deliver on-demand, scalable computing infrastructure, built on an underlying Hyper-V platform. You can mitigate local network failure, disk failure, and any planned downtime by using multiple virtual machines. Windows Azure implements this type of fault tolerance with Fault Domains, Update Domains, and Availability Sets:

- **Fault Domain**: This is closely equivalent to a rack of physical servers. It is defined by single points of failure, like the failure of a network switch, or the power unit for a rack of servers.

- **Update Domain**: This is used to mitigate a single point of failure, by ensuring that not all of the virtual machine instances are updated at the same time. An update domain's purpose is to ensure that when you or Microsoft is updating the OS, the availability of SharePoint continues.

- **Availability Set**: This maps the two different types of domains: fault domains and update domains. Adding multiple server instances to an Availability Set can give your organization the assurance that SharePoint is available and resilient against single points of failure. When you assign multiple virtual machines to an availability set, Windows Azure ensures that the virtual machine instances are assigned to different update domains. The following graphic illustrates the relationship between availability sets, fault domains, resource domains, and the virtual machines within each availability set:

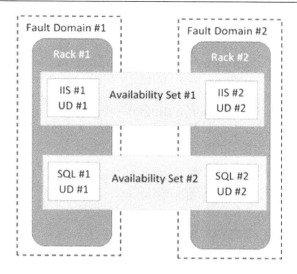

This diagram conceptually depicts SharePoint WFE and SQL resources in a single rack, protected by a fault domain. If one rack were to fail, the other will pick up the requests. Each resource is assigned an availability set, which protects the resource by assigning virtual machines to a fault domain and an update domain.

For more information on Azure Virtual Machines, visit `http://www.windowsazure.com/en-us/services/virtual-machines/`.

Load balancing

While fault and update domains can give us a level of redundancy and fault tolerance, load balancing is the mechanism that protects the performance of our SharePoint environment during peak times of high volume traffic.

Windows Azure provides the ability to create end-points which can act as load balancers to maintain high availability. For more information on the load balancing methods available in Windows Azure via Traffic Manager, visit `http://msdn.microsoft.com/en-us/library/windowsazure/dn339010.aspx`.

Storage

One of the ways in which Windows Azure implements storage is by using Binary Large Objects (BLOBs)—collections of binary information. To protect against hardware failures and to improve availability, every BLOB is replicated across three computers in a Windows Azure datacenter. The BLOB's data can also be copied to another Windows Azure datacenter in the same region, but at least 500 miles away. This copying, called geo-replication, happens within a few minutes of an update to the BLOB, and it is very useful for disaster recovery.

For more information on Azure Storage, visit `http://www.windowsazure.com/en-us/documentation/services/storage/`.

Hyper-V Recovery Manager

With Windows Azure Hyper-V Recovery Manager, your organization can coordinate the replication and recovery of private clouds to a secondary location through integration with System Center 2012. This service helps to automate the orderly recovery of virtual machines in the event of a site outage at the primary datacenter.

Please note that at the time of writing, Hyper-V Recovery Manager is a limited preview program only available to a small group of customers.

For more information on this service, please visit `http://www.windowsazure.com/en-us/services/recovery-manager/`.

Summary

This chapter gave you a good understanding of various different cloud approaches to DR, and also explained how DR/HA can be implemented by using native mechanisms from some of today's mainstream cloud providers. This chapter did not cover disaster recovery with respect to Office 365, as that is pretty apparent in Microsoft's SLAs and service continuity agreements (and should be with any SaaS offering). I've witnessed my share of failed SharePoint implementations and I would say that almost all of them could have been avoided by simply doing more strategic planning. This can't be overstated, particularly as it applies to disaster recovery and business continuity planning. And planning is even more important when integrating with cloud technologies, as another layer gets introduced into the mix. In any case, there are a couple of things that we hope you remember.

There is no "one-size-fits-all" disaster recovery plan or model. Despite the appearance of similarity in all of the participating technical tiers, and the same perceived desire for governance and continuity, you should assume that each organization's needs will be unique and will need to be uniquely addressed.

You won't get it right the first time. Which is not to say that you won't get close. Nonetheless, assume that you will follow an iterative approach, not only technically but also politically, as budgets, regulations, application, and process owners enter the fray. Once disaster recovery and continuity plans are defined, the processes are deployed and tested, and you think your solution is complete, prepare for the inevitability that the technology will change, and fast.

Cloud technology is evolving quickly. Whatever your DR implementation looks like today, be prepared to alter it as mainstream cloud providers release newer features and capabilities, and actually reduce costs (as often happens with AWS). In fact, organizations should consider some type of explicit, ongoing optimization contract either with their vendors or with designated internal departments. The purpose of this service contract should be to evaluate information technologies quarterly, to find in order to determine where processes can be optimized and costs reduced through the use of evolving and emerging cloud technologies.

The next chapter concludes this book, and puts together a structured starting approach, tying together all of the content presented in this book's other chapters.

10
Where to Start

This chapter wraps up the book's original objective, which is to empower you with the ability to plan, test, and deploy SharePoint Disaster Recovery procedures within your organization.

Building on the knowledge obtained from this book, such as backup and restore procedures, testing and maintenance, custom development DR approaches and considerations, this chapter's intent is to provide "sticking power" to this knowledge with a series of FAQs.

How to get my organization moving in the right direction

So you need to do some SharePoint DR planning, but aren't sure how to start Depending on the size of the task and the level of prior focus on **Business Continuity** (**BC**) or DR planning within your organization, this could involve anything from simply sprucing up your existing documentation to the overwhelming feat of creating new plan designs and implementations. If the latter is your situation, don't feel alone. There are many data center managers, IT executives, and application owners that feel like they're behind the 8-ball with their business continuity and disaster planning efforts. Rest assure and know that with the right steps as outlined in this book, you can get things moving forward in the right direction.

One of the approaches that the authors recommend is the 60-40 rule, which means that you should start out and by identifying goals and objectives that are only 60 percent of where you would ideally wish to see the end-state starting with start with a roadmap with dates and deliveries.

How to sell DR to senior management

How do we, as IT professionals, sell the importance of DR to senior management, given this is going to require additional funding and budgets that may not be available?

Firstly don't use the word "disaster". Management immediately thinks of natural catastrophes. Use the term, "IT recovery" but if you don't want to stray too far from conventional parlance, you could always go with..."IT disaster recovery".

Start talking about IT DR in terms of risk mitigation. Most senior executives understand the concept of risk very well. You can leverage this to your advantage by helping them frame up the issue in terms of risks they will pay to mitigate versus risks they are willing to accept.

Make sure senior management understands the benefits of IT DR, but use the benefits they're interested in, such as the following:

- Gain competitive advantage
- Increase revenue
- Gain the ability to predict business performance
- Meet supply chain demands
- Meet regulatory and compliance requirements
- Meet SLAs
- Meet fiduciary duties to shareholders

Make sure senior management understands that if you're already backing up your data, it is not a much of a leap to IT DR.

 You might want to spell it out for your CXO. Backing up your data onto tape, disk, or cloud is protecting your data. However, to make certain that data can be recovered in the event of an outage, you need to have more than 1's and 0's on your medium of choice. You need to have an infrastructure that mirrors your production environment at your recovery site. No one wants backups; they want recovery.

Let them know that this will cost them SharePoint dollars.

I feel the SharePoint end users don't care about SharePoint DR. Is this true?

You are right! They don't care, but they should. This is particularly frustrating when months have been spent drafting, refining, and testing the DR plan only for it to be stored in someone's e-mail folder which probably will not be accessible on the day that it is needed.

Lack of attention is the single element that can sink your master DR plan before it ever gets a chance to shine. This is usually because of the reasons explained next.

Why was I not told?

Believe it or not, most employees believe this subject should be the responsibility of the IT department, yes whether it is a deleted file or a complete power failure in the building. They just assume someone will take care of the SharePoint site and that the backups will work and it is business as usual. They don't understand that they may have a role in preventing content from going offline and allowing the team to be collaborating together. This is because they have not been made aware of the techniques and approaches they can use to recover from a full or partial meltdown of a SharePoint environment.

In 2013, InformationWeek conducted a State of Storage Survey and found the following details:

- Less than 50 percent of survey respondents had a disaster recovery and business continuity strategy in place and tested it regularly
- 40 percent had a Disaster Recovery plan in place but rarely tested it
- 20% had no plan

If possible, engage the company end users by hosting a lunch and learn or brown bag awareness training. This should include what users should do in the event that they can't do their jobs with content not available in SharePoint. This should include explicit printed instructions for remote working, and how to report an outage if the e-mail is also down. This is explained in *Chapter 8, Disaster Recovery Techniques for End Users*.

If you really want to test the system, schedule a deliberate outage over the weekend and build a lessons-learned journal. This immediately identifies knowledge/skill gaps in the recovery steps of the team.

The word "disaster" is not understood

It's not Bruce Willis saving New York from the bad guys (I suppose this would be a recovery), but rather SharePoint DR more often involves power outages due to various facility incidents, or data loss from DNS entry changes, or just general clumsiness of employees deleting a site or web applications accidentally. These aren't one-time events but rather things that are definitely going to happen—maybe not today, maybe not next week, but it's predictable that it will happen. CIOs know and understand this, because they have been around IT, but your employees typically don't understand or don't want to understand.

This is where awareness sessions provide an understanding of what could happen and what steps need to be done to kick off the recovery process. Include several scenarios that people can understand and are actionable.

At times I can be the last to know of a business activity with SharePoint

Welcome to the IT department, often known as the anti-sales department or the land or no, IT must be aligned with the business and always communicating with it, so the business units are supported. The authors of SharePoint DR plans overlooked business-critical processes simply because they don't realize they are essential. This can include, but is not limited to the following points:

- External data sources that are being used in SharePoint
- Installed third-party web parts that are not listed
- Exchange integration

It is easier said than done, but IT needs to stay on top of what mission is critical this week.

I have written the DR plan but will it work?

If your DR plan is a 30-page document that has been written up by a sole individual and e-mailed to the IT department with the hope that everyone is going to read, understand, and be able to act on its contents, then you can pretty much guarantee that your DR plan will fail.

Writing the plan is the first step, but the plan needs to be continuously shared with other team members and when the plan is implemented, communications and updates must continue as stated in *Chapter 1, Planning and Key Concepts – What Not to Forget*, and *Chapter 2, Creating, Testing, and Maintaining the DR Plan*. Keys are the defined roles within your DR plan, with who is responsible for the backup and restoration of the technologies such as Windows Server, the SQL Server databases, and the communications to the organization.

Another important aspect of a DR plan is the practice of testing the recovery process which obviously confirms that the plan works.

When a recovery is first performed in a test or real situation, chances are that it will not work fully. There will probably be time delays, system accounts not working, forgotten passwords, access issues, and the list goes on. The point is that practice makes perfect, and performing practice scenarios a few times a year is essential to a fully functional DR plan.

> *"Practice does not make perfect. Only perfect practice makes perfect."*
>
> *— Vincent Thomas "Vince" Lombardi*

A successful SharePoint DR plan is ultimately the responsibility of the IT management team, and it is often overlooked as an activity to do on a list of priorities. It is essential that it needs to be rehearsed to be executed flawlessly.

Management must declare a DR plan as a department initiative and mission critical and review the steps and resources periodically to make a DR plan rock solid.

If writing and communicating a DR plan becomes a passive activity, then the DR plan is not going to work, or is going to have very unpredictable results on the day that it is required.

Remember that what gets seen gets measured. So when the action plan of how to get the DR plan operating at an acceptable level is agreed upon, share it with the department, business, and other relevant management team in order to get their buy-in and co-operation. Make sure everyone is on the same page, working towards the common vision and goals of making a DR plan a success.

What are the key skills that are required for a DR plan to work?

It is more than just technical skills. Often, SharePoint implementations are not completely thought out, and if the technical portion has gone viral within an organization, management needs to step in and perhaps identify some risks and DR procedures that need to be put in place.

Allocating appropriate resources to the plan is critical. A successful plan will take many hours. This activity should be viewed as an infrastructure project.

Depending on what SharePoint is being used for, the skill set should involve the following:

- **Technical skills**: SQL Server and SharePoint administrator — people critical to performing the work.
- **IT management**: people accountable for the DR plan.
- **Solid technical writer**: a writer who is thorough and comprehensive. Most technical folks unfortunately do not have this skill. This is an unfortunate reality.

The job title, SharePoint administrator, is a loosely-defined role. There is a lot more to it than just creating groups and site collections. This person must be proficient with SQL Server, IIS, content databases, and Active Directory.

The technology mentioned in the last sentence of the previous paragraph does not mention SharePoint. The SharePoint administrator must be proficient with these technologies.

How do you write up the perfect DR documentation?

Writing the DR plan is generally not performed in a single clean swoop of activity, so sort out the good, the bad, and the ugly. Fix the obvious first, such as system account information, server names, and disk space.

Good technical documentation is a challenge because at one extreme, technical documentation is often written by technical experts who dislike writing and give it as little effort as possible, with no formal criteria. Or at the other extreme, the documentation is written by artisan technical writers who lack the formal technical criteria needed to evaluate the effectiveness of the product in view of the needs of the readers.

The previous chapters of this book have stated what is needed in a DR plan. This question really asks how you write the required information to an acceptable level where the documentation is readable and actionable. In essence, a technical resource can read the document and know what steps are required to be performed, by whom, and when.

 Writing clear technical documentation is challenging because the technical personnel in IT are normally spending most day reacting to support issues and therefore have little down time to write long and detailed documentation. Allocating time may need to be approved by senior management.

For this to occur, the authors recommend the following measures:

- Have regularly schedule meetings with all parties involved, in order to ensure common understanding.
- Set dates for deliverables to create urgency with regard to when goals and milestones need to be met and by whom.
- Identify an owner for every related technology. This could be the same person for multiple processes. State a backup owner as well.
- Obtain sign off from management at every milestone.
- Set a completion date for each stage.

 The bullet point "Obtain sign off from management" is key, as this holds the responsible parties accountable.

What should consist in the structure of good technical documentation?

Good technical documentation should include the following structure:

Outline

Develop an outline for each document that shows how the document is structured. This will save a lot of time in trying to figure out what the document should include. The outline should follow a logical sequence, with outline items indented so that similar or related items are at the same level. This outline is stated in *Chapter 2, Creating, Testing, and Maintaining the DR Plan.*

Content

There is a belief in the corporate world that no one reads documentation anymore, and this is partly true. The documentation must be easy to understand and targeted to the technical reader. The IT department has little interest in the business value of a mission critical SharePoint application.

Also, reference external sources which may have detailed explanation of a technology or a process that a technical reader is not too familiar with.

 A picture is worth a thousand words. A link to a YouTube video could be a lot more informative.

For task-oriented documents, consider using the play script procedure writing style.

 Play script writing is based on the concept that a procedure is like a stage play with the action moving from one person to another in a defined time sequence. Each procedure is written like the script of a play showing each of the actors and their actions they perform in time sequence.

Because of complexity, technical documentation is often out-of-date; play script procedures are written in the language of the end users and document the practical step-by-step issues that users face when carrying out their tasks. The main thrust of the play script method is to cull policy and general descriptive material, leaving behind the step-by-step detail of how to carry out the procedure.

This approach is really what the reader wants to understand: how activity flows from one event to the next, and how to work in a coordinated team.

Graphics

Flow chart graphics show the flow of relevant items and make content easier to read. Other relevant graphics might include screenshots of the technology.

Review

All documents should go through a review process by team members who are acquainted with the technical subject in which you are writing about, and they should provide feedback. This will hopefully reduce misunderstanding of the steps when the document will be referenced in a real recovery situation.

Distribution

Distribute the document to the intended audience. It is recommended that you also print the document and inform all users the location of it so that it can be referenced in the case of a power failure.

Can this whole process be outsourced to an external party?

Not really. There are plenty of companies that provide this kind of service, but it is not recommended to have a third party spend weeks writing up documentation which is really an "insurance policy" in case things go wrong.

As discussed in this chapter, writing the documentation is only the first step of a DR plan. It also needs to be set up, improved, and executed.

These resources need to be internal where management has direct authority over, them rather than through an account manager of the vendor. The DR plan needs to be internalized versus an adaptation of someone's ideal process or conceptual notion.

Do not delegate this role to an employee (or a summer intern...yes this has been witnessed) who has never written a complicated technical publication before, and who may lack the authority and leverage to do it well. Ironically, the writing of online documentation is often entrusted to the same administrators who write cryptic screens and messages that frustrate users who thump their keyboards in desperation.

Can implementing a DR strategy really help my career?

Well, this is not the intent of a DR plan, but if resources are an integral part of the process then they are essential to the IT operations.

On the day when they DR plan is required to be triggered into action, the IT team will be seen as the super hero.

What methods should I use to keep upper management informed on the DR Program?

Keep it on a single page, and that is it. Perhaps use a two-dimensional matrix with color coding of Red, Yellow, and Green indicating risks and threats, as these may need additional funding. The eyes will be drawn to those shaded in red.

Most senior managers just want an overview, so save the details for the line managers.

Further reading

Microsoft SQL Server 2012 Performance Tuning Cookbook: http://www.packtpub.com/microsoft-sql-server-2012-performance-tuning-cookbook/book.

Microsoft SQL Server 2008 R2 Administration Cookbook: http://www.packtpub.com/microsoft-sql-server-2008-r2-administration-cookbook/book.

SQL Server 2012 with PowerShell V3 Cookbook: http://www.packtpub.com/sql-server-2012-with-powershell-v3-cookbook/book.

The Art of Technical Documentation: http://www.amazon.com/The-Technical-Documentation-Second-Edition/dp/155558182X.

Summary

The big win of this book is that there should be no surprises for either the business or IT, when the DR plan does not or does work. In short, plan for the best and be prepared for the worst.

In this chapter, you have been introduced to some concepts and ideas of how to apply the knowledge gained from this book with your DR initiative.

As ever, we hope that you will be as impressed as we are with Microsoft's SharePoint 2013 backup and restore procedures, and understand the challenges, pitfalls, and opportunities of deploying and managing a DR plan. More than that, we hope that you have enjoyed not just this chapter, but also the book, and that it has helped you further understand SharePoint from a DR standpoint.

With any technology initiative. you end up with one of two things: the results of a project or the reasons why you don't have the results. Results don't have to be explained; they just are the way they are.

All the writers of this book believe a great technical book should do three things: educate, share, and engage. Good luck!

Appendix

Every organization that is using SharePoint for mission-critical applications has a DR plan, as well as situations where it just has not worked. The appendix of the book highlights some of the battle scars of the DR process—war stories that the authors of the book have witnessed, and educates the reader with some amusing anecdotes.

The appendix covers:

- Worst practices
- Horror stories that the authors have witnessed
- How and why assumptions can sink a DR plan
- Real world scenarios for consideration
- Tools for consideration
- Useful references
- Appendix naming conventions

Worst and best practices

This section covers worst practices which, believe it or not, are quite common in the world of DR. You should read each vignette and avoid the scenario.

We can snapshot our servers

Taking a VMware snapshot of a server is only good as long as the snapshot is retained. As it ages, the differences tracked consume an increasing proportion of storage. This can slow down the server as well.

Being able to restore a server image is of limited use if the database images cannot be rolled back to the same point in time. Having a server rollback without a database rollback can lead to an inconsistent and inoperable farm. That is because the database schema needs to be in a valid range supported by the server software.

The DIY Approach

The PowerShell scripts can be viewed as an inexpensive way to build a comprehensive backup of databases and servers, but if they are home grown they will need to be clearly documented and they will not be supported by a 24 hour support line.

 There is a reason why complicated processes like payroll and backup software exist.

We have a production SharePoint Farm

If there is only one SharePoint farm, there's no place to test changes. Any production change, no matter how safe it is assumed to be, can wreak havoc on a farm. Any release needs to be tested in an isolated test environment prior to deployment to production.

Examples of SharePoint disasters that can corrupt a production environment include:

- Running out of disk space during a recovery. This is not always easy to estimate because temporary files are constantly created
- A deployment or uninstall leaving non-functional references in `web.config`
- Orphaned feature references

 If there is only one farm, it is a development SharePoint farm and not a production farm.

Our DR servers can be undersized

Under-sizing a server can be a cost-effective strategy, until it fails. Insufficient storage can cause a hard-failure. Insufficient resource, such as RAM, can cripple a SharePoint farm. At the very least, be sure to test any undersized hardware.

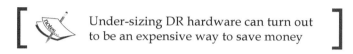 Under-sizing DR hardware can turn out to be an expensive way to save money

Oversights in a DR recovery plan

This section, lists some oversights in SharePoint DR plans that IT should know what to do with. We aren't just talking about storing all the DR documentation in SharePoint, we are talking about the very technology that is being recovered.

Invalid testing

A Cincinnati data center tested their power failover to a diesel generator backup, and it always worked. One day the power went out, and the backup generators failed. It turned out the fuel pump for the generator was on the grid and not on the UPS (Uninterruptable Power Supply).

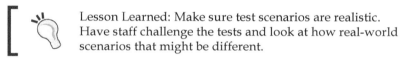 Lesson Learned: Make sure test scenarios are realistic. Have staff challenge the tests and look at how real-world scenarios that might be different.

No failback plan

A New Jersey financial firm had a robust DR plan. When hurricane Sandy hit, the firm decided to stay offline for a week, rather than fail over to the DR site, as they had not worked out how to fail back.

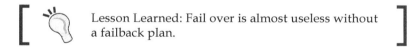 Lesson Learned: Fail over is almost useless without a failback plan.

Horror stories that the authors have witnessed

Every IT veteran has a horror story; the following are just a few horror stories that the authors have witnessed.

Backups only

Many organizations have suffered from this simple oversight. Backups are scheduled, and methodically taken. When a restore is needed, the backups are found to be non-functional. Due to be bad media or faulty backup configuration.

 Lesson Learned: A backup has no value if it can't be restored. A DR plan has to include testing a restore.

Pixar's near loss of Toy Story 2

A worker at Pixar accidentally ran a command that wiped out 30 years of work on the movie *Toy Story 2*. The local nightly backup had been silently failing for over a month. In the end, a backup was found on a director's laptop.

 Lessons learned: Test the backups. Ensure they can be restored.

This is explained further in the following link:

http://www.zetta.net/blog/pixar-deleted-toy-story-2-cloud-disaster-recovery-hero/

SharePoint backup encrypted

For security reasons, a hedge fund encrypt their backups. Sounds good until they tried to do a restore. The encryption keys were on the backup.

 Lessons learnt: Test the restore process. Practice makes it perfect.

Solution retraction caused web application failure

Retracting a solution can cause web applications including Central Administration to fail. This occurred when uninstalling an older version of a great tool (Idera SharePoint Manager) and also trying to uninstall the SP Diagnostic toolkit.

 Lessons learnt: Try retracting first in development.

How and why assumptions can sink a DR plan

Assumptions are the foundation upon which failure can occur. As part of the DR plan every assumption needs to be questioned:

- To what environment would recovery occur?
- Can we gain access to our DR site in the event of a disaster?
- Will key staff be reachable in the event of a disaster?
- Will key staff be able to commute in the event of a disaster?
- Will internet access be available to key staff during a disaster?
- If a disaster is widespread, will many companies converge onto and overwhelm the planned DR site?

Small changes still have the ability to prevent Central Administration from coming up

Deploying or retracting a web part that is only loaded on a single page can cause catastrophic failure. One example of when this can occur is when trying to perform a retract via the Central Administration user interface of a SharePoint solution that is deployed to Central Administration itself. For any such solution, Central Administration happily tries to retract the solution and it fails. The author ran into this when trying to uninstall Powerpivotwebapp.wsp. The solution was to perform the retract via PowerShell. During several initial retract attempts, the Central Administration in production was rendered inaccessible. All attempts to repair Central Administration failed. Luckily, rollback was possible.

 Lesson learnt: Have a development environment identical to production, and release through development, staging, and production, with change requirement documentation signed.

Real-world scenarios for consideration

This section of the appendix outlines some points of failure and suggestions for you to consider.

User overwrites a file

Versioning is great, but if a user uploads with overwrite, in some cases this creates a new document. This happened to Sudip about a year ago. In explorer mode. It required a full content DB restore to Dev. In-location restore was not an option, as that would roll all content back.

The feature retract failure

Feature fails on retract across: farm and orphaned GUIDs; perhaps SharePoint server and configuration DB out of sync with content DBs and GAC, Registry, and Web.config. Other areas that can get out sync are IIS configuration (IIS Metabase), SharePoint webroot folders, and certificate stores. Note registry syncs with the config DB (there are PowerShell commands to force a resync in some cases). Third party apps can touch standard XML files, customize site definitions (webtemp.xml), iFilters (like PDFs), workflows, custom fields, custom content type definitions and so on.

Restore a service application

Imagine a need to restore BCS, search, or MMS. Imagine an MMS rollback that results in recent terms, that are used in content DBs, disappearing. This includes references used within a content DB, as well as the service application linkage to its own databases. Restore has to include the proxy connection.

Restore wipes key drive information

Best practice is to store all code and install packages on each SharePoint server. If a rollback or uninstall fails, the reinstallation can sometimes restore the farm to a working state. Server rollback would cause these to roll back as well, which is not always what is desired. Best practice is to supplement server storage of releases with a dedicated drive for such static install packages so that they don't get rolled back.

Service application DBs

Depending on what was changed, Secure Store entries can be out of sync, as can BCS items, search managed crawl properties, or if a server snapshot was restored but the databases are not, or vise versa.

Search out of date on restore

Imagine a rollback of either content DBs or search; the search index can be ahead of the older content DB restore, having references to documents that were added after the content restore point. Or the incremental crawl won't pick up on Content DB change log entries after a restore point. The short answer is a full crawl after a restore.

Non-SharePoint

Consider any additional IIS web services for customizations. SharePoint Central Administration backups are unaware of these additions as they exist outside SharePoint, and their backup/restore needs to be taken into account.

Servers in sync

If there are multiple servers in the farm, they need to be chronologically in sync; if one server is restored but not another, the server GACs will be different. If the servers are not consistent, then users who are being served by one server may receive different results than users who are being served by another server.

IIS

IIS settings need backup/restore consideration. At the very least, the following settings need to be documented as part of the DR plan:

- Application pool settings, including service accounts
- HTTP compression settings
- Time-out settings
- Custom ISAPI filters
- Computer domain membership
- **Internet Protocol security (IPsec)** settings
- Network Load Balancing settings
- Host header entries
- **Secure Sockets Layer (SSL)** certificates
- Dedicated IP address settings

SharePoint configurations that need to be in sync across environments are as follows:

- Application pool settings, including service accounts (all accounts that run as Web applications, including the crawler account and the search account)
- Alternate access mapping settings
- Farm-level search settings
- External service connection settings
- Workflow management settings
- E-mail settings

Doomsday DR

Consider the following scenario. There is a major problem with your current live SharePoint environment and everything goes wrong. All there are, is some new hardware, DVDs, and a set of backups if you are lucky. Could this be rebuilt from scratch within a reasonable timeframe? Would all of the necessary documentation be in place, detailing the steps to take in order to rebuild your SharePoint environment? Granted, this is an extreme scenario, but once the basics are in place, it makes sense to devote some thought to the more extreme scenarios.

Tools for consideration

There are limits to the capabilities within SharePoint that are addressed by third party vendors. These can blur the line with backup/recovery software. Below is a sample of some vendor offerings to be aware of in the planning stage:

Vendor	Product	Site
Idera	SharePoint Backup	http://www.idera.com/
Quest	Recovery Manager	http://www.quest.com/
AvePoint	DocAve	http://www.avepoint.com/
NeverFail	Continuity Protection	http://www.neverfailgroup.com/

Useful references

A list of references that will be useful is as follows:

- *Richard Harbridge: SharePoint glossary*: http://www.rharbridge.com/?page_id=60

- *SharePoint high availability and Disaster Recovery*: http://www.slideshare.net/thomasvochten/sharepoint-high-availability-disaster-recovery

- *SharePoint 2013 Business Continuity DR: Management Features*: http://www.youtube.com/watch?v=DvRSVbhydyU

- *What SharePoint 2013 means for the data center*: http://www.computerworld.com/s/article/9234922/What_SharePoint_2013_means_for_the_data_center

- *SharePoint best practices*: http://social.technet.microsoft.com/wiki/contents/articles/12438.sharepoint-2013-best-practices.aspx

- *Common DR terms*: http://www.binomial.com/resources/glossary.php

Naming conventions

This part of the appendix relates to *Chapter 6, Working with Data Sizing and Data Structure,* and provides basic naming conventions to consider when adopting in best practices. These are as follows:

- Avoid GUIDs at all costs. It is too easy to fat-finger a database name with embedded GUIDs during a recovery operation.

- Avoid blanks. Including a blank in a database name limits the syntax of scripted backup/recovery operations, increasing the possibility of error.

- Avoid underscores in file names. Underscores increase database name length and are easy to confuse with blanks during the time pressure of a recovery operation.

- Leave "DB" and "database" out of the name. Keeping database names short and sweet simplifies management.

- Use capital letters to highlight the start of words (this is sometimes referred to as CamelCase). This makes database names easier to read, even though programmatic references to database names are case-insensitive.

- Use consistent descriptions when associating a database with a specific web app, and service app. This improves the ease of an Administrator finding the correct database for recovery.

- References to Production versus Development are not necessary, to keep names short.

- References to SharePoint version are not necessary, to keep naming short.

- References to "SharePoint" are unnecessary, especially for a dedicated SQL Server, to keep names short.

- Leave the obscure WSS SharePoint convention for content databases, and instead use "Content" at the start of the database name. That's clearer for DBAs who are not versed in the mysterious acronyms of SharePoint.

The following is a proposed syntax for structuring database names, followed by a table explaining them in more detail:

```
[Major Application][Type] [Minor Application] [Specific]
```

Component	Description	Sample Values
[Major Application]	Major category of application	[left blank for SharePoint] MSPS (for MS Project Server)
[Type]	Category or type of database, based on primary system using the database	Content ServiceApp
[Minor Application]	Can be a service application	PerformancePoint ManagedMetadata
[Specific]	Can describe each of multiple service app DBs. Description of use of content DB for web app	CentralAdmin

The following code contains examples for structured database name:

```
Default: Search_Connector_CrawlStoreDB_4040b7300e9e42779edb3e6b926be5a7
New: ServiceApp_SearchConnectorCrawlStore

Default: SharePoint_AdminContent_ff35d171-482c-4f9d-8305-a4a259ec1a15
New: Content_CentralAdmin

Default: wss_content_eaee9d8f-ed75-4a56-bad3-5abf232b4f66
New: Content_ DIV_HR

Default: StateService_0f2a42e8b90d4c60830ca442e753de13
New: ServiceApp_State
```

Index

Binary Large Objects (BLOBs) 101, 111, 116
BlobCache 144
Business Connectivity Services. *See* BCS
Business Continuity (BC) 217
business continuity plan. *See* BCP
Business data connectivity service 100
business impact analysis (BIA) 37

C

Central Administration 162
Central Administration GUI
  used, for Content database backup 112
  used, for Content database restore 113
  used, for Customizations backup 116
  used, for Customizations restore 117, 118
  used, for Farm backup 91-93
  used, for Farm configuration backup 102
  used, for Farm configuration restore 103
  used, for Farm restore 94-98
  used, for Service application backup 108
  used, for Service application restore 109
  used, for site collection backup 120
  used, for sites backup 124-126
  used, for Web application backup 105
  used, for Web application restore 106
Certificates 100
change management
  about 167
  constant, ways 173
  software development life cycle 169, 170
  source code control 168
  supporting farms, using 171
Change Management Process 167
Change Request 167
Charts of PowerShell commands
  URL 70
claims-based authentication 107
  URL 101
Cloud App Model 173, 174
Cloud computing 22
cloud DR
  common concerns 202, 203
  general approaches 205, 206
cloud models
  Infrastructure as a Service (IaaS) 22
  Platform as a Service (PaaS) 22

Software as a Service (SaaS) 22
Cloud responsibility
  about 203
  IaaS 203
  PaaS 204
  SaaS 203
Code 161
Cold standby 15
Cold standby DR strategy
  about 15
  advantages 15
  disadvantages 15
cold standby recovery 17
Comma Separated Value. *See* CSV
compression 127
Configuration database 100
Configuration Management 164
content
  about 224
  retrieving 187
Content database backup
  caveats and considerations 115, 116
  Central Administration GUI used 112
  PowerShell used 112
  SQL server tools used 115
  SQL server tools used, URL 115
  to snapshots, URL 115
  URL 122
content database growth
  backup plan 152-155
  managing 134, 135, 148
  quotas, setting 148-150
  rebalancing 150
  recovery, tiering 156
  restore plan 152-155
  version retention, restricting 150
Content database restore
  caveats and considerations 115, 116
  Central Administration GUI used 113
  PowerShell used 113, 114
  SQL server tools used 115
  SQL server tools used, URL 115
  unattached content databases used 114, 115
  URL 122
content database size
  about 134
  determining 139

W

Thank you for buying
Microsoft SharePoint 2013
Disaster Recovery Guide

About Packt Publishing

Packt, pronounced 'packed', published its first book "Mastering phpMyAdmin for Effective MySQL Management" in April 2004 and subsequently continued to specialize in publishing highly focused books on specific technologies and solutions.

Our books and publications share the experiences of your fellow IT professionals in adapting and customizing today's systems, applications, and frameworks. Our solution based books give you the knowledge and power to customize the software and technologies you're using to get the job done. Packt books are more specific and less general than the IT books you have seen in the past. Our unique business model allows us to bring you more focused information, giving you more of what you need to know, and less of what you don't.

Packt is a modern, yet unique publishing company, which focuses on producing quality, cutting-edge books for communities of developers, administrators, and newbies alike. For more information, please visit our website: www.packtpub.com.

About Packt Enterprise

In 2010, Packt launched two new brands, Packt Enterprise and Packt Open Source, in order to continue its focus on specialization. This book is part of the Packt Enterprise brand, home to books published on enterprise software – software created by major vendors, including (but not limited to) IBM, Microsoft and Oracle, often for use in other corporations. Its titles will offer information relevant to a range of users of this software, including administrators, developers, architects, and end users.

Writing for Packt

We welcome all inquiries from people who are interested in authoring. Book proposals should be sent to author@packtpub.com. If your book idea is still at an early stage and you would like to discuss it first before writing a formal book proposal, contact us; one of our commissioning editors will get in touch with you.

We're not just looking for published authors; if you have strong technical skills but no writing experience, our experienced editors can help you develop a writing career, or simply get some additional reward for your expertise.

**Learning Search-driven Application
Development with SharePoint 2013**

ISBN: 978-1-78217-100-3   Paperback: 106 pages

Build optimum search-driven applications using
SharePoint 2013's new and improved search engine

1. Create search-driven applications using the
   new SharePoint 2013 enterprise search engine

2. Learn how to respond intelligently to user's
   search queries using Query Rules

3. Filled with helpful tips, diagrams, and practical
   examples to make your organization's search
   experience smarter

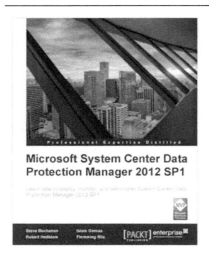

**Microsoft System Center Data
Protection Manager 2012 SP1**

ISBN: 978-1-84968-630-3   Paperback: 328 pages

Learn how to deploy, monitor, and administer
System Center Data Protection Manager 2012 SP1

1. Practical guidance that will help you get
   the most out of Microsoft System Center
   Data Protection Manager 2012

2. Gain insight into deploying, monitoring,
   and administering System Center Data
   Protection Manager 2012 from a team of
   Microsoft MVPs

3. Learn the various methods and best practices
   for administrating and using Microsoft System
   Center Data Protection Manager 2012

Please check **www.PacktPub.com** for information on our titles

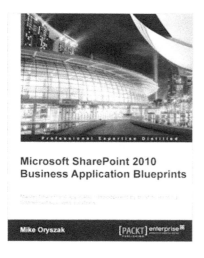

Microsoft SharePoint 2010
Business Application Blueprints

Microsoft SharePoint 2010 Business Application Blueprints

ISBN: 978-1-84968-360-9   Paperback: 282 pages

Master SharePoint application development by building exciting SharePoint business solutions

1. Instant SharePoint – Build nine exciting SharePoint business solutions

2. Expand your knowledge of the SharePoint platform so that you can tailor the sample solutions to your requirements

3. Learn how the different development techniques can be used in various situations to support both client side and server side development to solve different problems in different environments.

Microsoft SharePoint for Business Executives:
Q&A Handbook

Microsoft SharePoint for Business Executives: Q&A Handbook

ISBN: 978-1-84968-610-5   Paperback: 236 pages

100 Essential Questions and Answers about SharePoint 2010 for Executives considering SharePoint deployments

1. Forget lengthy technical SharePoint guides more suited for hands-on technical staff; get equipped with the knowledge of SharePoint's business potential before deployment

2. Get to grips with SharePoint governance, the Cloud, staffing, development and much more from a business perspective in this book and e-book

3. An essential SharePoint Pocket Guide with useful Q&As for every business executive deliberating over SharePoint implementation

Please check **www.PacktPub.com** for information on our titles

www.ingramcontent.com/pod-product-compliance
Lightning Source LLC
LaVergne TN
LVHW062309060326
832902LV00013B/2131